A CROCHETED
Garden of Afghans

WELCOME TO MY GARDEN

MW00995766

LEISURE ARTS, INC.
Little Rock, Arkansas

EDITORIAL STAFF

Vice President and Editor-at-Large: Anne Van Wagner Childs
Vice President and Editor-in-Chief: Sandra Graham Case
Director of Designer Relations: Debra Nettles
Editorial Director: Susan Frantz Wiles
Publications Director: Susan White Sullivan
Creative Art Director: Gloria Bearden
Photography Director: Karen Smart Hall
Art Operations Director: Jeff Curtis

PRODUCTION

Managing Editor: Valesha M. Kirksey
Technical Editor: Linda Luder
Senior Instructional Editor: Sarah J. Green
Instructional Editor: Susan Carter

EDITORIAL

Managing Editor: Suzie Puckett
Associate Editor: Stacey Marshall
Assistant Editors: Susan McManus Johnson and Taryn L. Stewart

ART

Graphics Art Director: Rhonda Hodge Shelby
Senior Graphics Illustrator: Lora Puls
Graphics Illustrator: Wendy Willets
Color Technician: Mark Hawkins
Photography Stylists: Tiffany Huffman and
   Janna Laughlin
Staff Photographer: Russell Ganser
Publishing Systems Administrator: Becky Riddle
Publishing Systems Assistants: Myra S. Means and
   Chris Wertenberger

BUSINESS STAFF

Publisher: Rick Barton
Vice President, Finance: Tom Siebenmorgen
Director of Corporate Planning and Development:
   Laticia Mull Cornett
Vice President, Retail Marketing: Bob Humphrey
Retail Marketing Director: Margaret Sweetin
Vice President, Sales: Ray Shelgosh
Vice President, National Accounts: Pam Stebbins
Vice President, Operations: Jim Dittrich
Comptroller, Operations: Rob Thieme
Retail Customer Service Manager: Wanda Price
Print Production Manager: Fred F. Pruss

Softcover ISBN 1-57486-216-2

10 9 8 7 6

A CROCHETER'S
Garden of Afghans

If you love flowers, you won't be able to resist the nature-inspired wraps in A Crocheter's Garden of Afghans. We've chosen four dozen afghans from our archives for this exciting collection. Whether you're a seasoned crocheter or just getting started, you'll find the perfect project for your level of skill. You can whip up a granny square wrap in just a few days, or take your time with one of the more intricate designs.

You'll find afghans "picked" right from the garden — featuring posies, roses, poppies, and more — in three inviting sections. Turn to Welcome to My Garden to find fabulous floral throws. Come and Sit a Spell presents a variety of cozy wraps, and Bringing the Outdoors In boasts projects that will introduce the beauty of nature into every room of your home.

So settle into a comfortable chair and thumb through the pages of this enchanting volume … and let us whisk you away to a fantastic garden of crocheted delights!

*F*or mine is just a little
old-fashioned garden where
the flowers come together
to praise the Lord and teach
all who look upon them
to do likewise.

— CELIA LAIGHTON THAXTER

Welcome
to my garden

contents

Come and sit a spell

Bringing the outdoors in

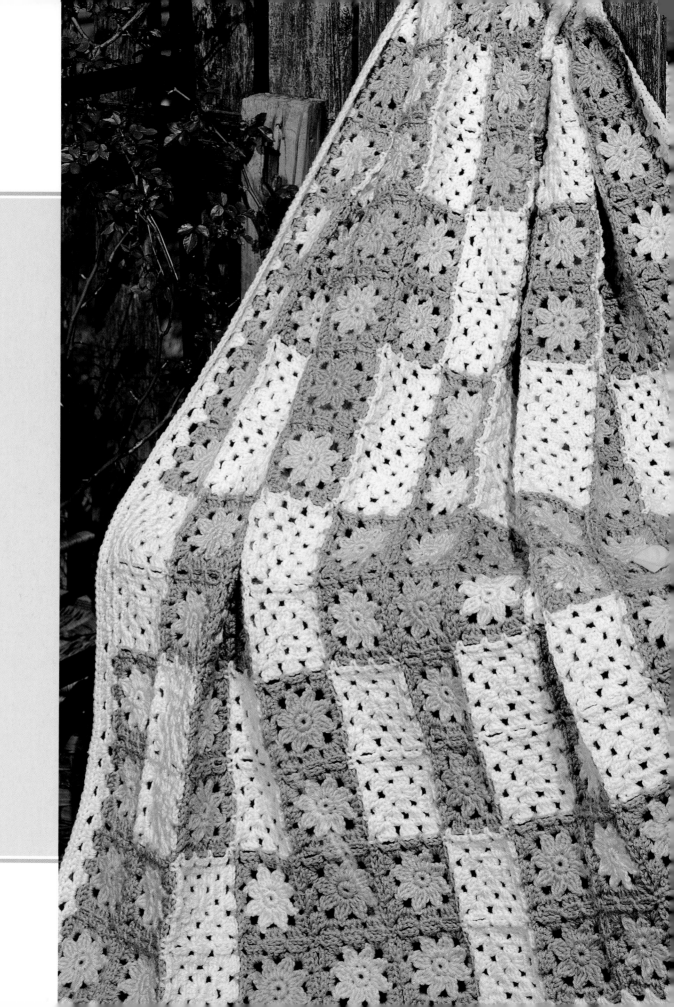

Welcome to my garden

Nothing compares to the glorious
beauty of nature. Flowers in full bloom stir
the soul and bring serenity to those who take
the time to enjoy them. Be it dahlias, daisies,
sunflowers, or zinnias that make you smile,
you're sure to find a favorite or two to
add to your "bouquet" of afghans.

Country Checks

Finished Size: 45" x 56"

MATERIALS
Worsted Weight Yarn:
Ecru - 33 ounces, (940 grams, 1,925 yards)
Green - 16 ounces, (450 grams, 930 yards)
Crochet hook, size H (5.00 mm) **or** size needed
for gauge

GAUGE SWATCH: 2¼" square
Work same as First Square.

FIRST SQUARE
With Ecru, ch 4; join with slip st to form a ring.

Rnd 1 (Right side)**:** Ch 3 **(counts as first dc, now
and throughout)**, 2 dc in ring, (ch 2, 3 dc in ring)
3 times, hdc in first dc to form last ch-2 sp:
4 ch-2 sps.

Note: Loop a short piece of yarn around any stitch
to mark Rnd 1 as **right** side.

Rnd 2: Ch 3, (2 dc, ch 2, 3 dc) in last ch-2 sp
made, ch 1, ★ (3 dc, ch 2, 3 dc) in next ch-2 sp,
ch 1; repeat from ★ 2 times **more**; join with slip st
to first dc, finish off: 8 sps.

ADDITIONAL SQUARES
Following Placement Diagram, make Squares
using color indicated.

The method used to connect the Squares is a
no-sew joining also known as "join-as-you-go".
After the First Square is made, each remaining
Square is worked through Rnd 1, then crocheted
together as Rnd 2 is worked.

Work same as First Square through Rnd 1:
4 ch-2 sps.

Rnd 2 (Joining rnd)**:** Using Placement Diagram as
a guide, work One or Two Side Joining **(Fig. 10,
page 144)**, arranging Squares into 20 vertical strips
of 25 Squares each.

ONE SIDE JOINING
Rnd 2 (Joining rnd)**:** Ch 3, (2 dc, ch 2, 3 dc) in last
ch-2 sp made, ch 1, (3 dc, ch 2, 3 dc) in next
ch-2 sp, ch 1, 3 dc in next ch-2 sp, ch 1, holding
Squares with **wrong** sides together, slip st in corner
sp on **adjacent Square**, ch 1, 3 dc in same ch-2 sp
on **new Square**, ch 1, slip st in next ch-1 sp on
adjacent Square, 3 dc in next ch-2 sp on **new
Square**, ch 1, slip st in next corner sp on **adjacent
Square**, ch 1, 3 dc in same ch-2 sp on **new
Square**, ch 1; join with slip st to first dc, finish off.

TWO SIDE JOINING
Rnd 2 (Joining rnd)**:** Ch 3, (2 dc, ch 2, 3 dc) in last
ch-2 sp made, ch 1, 3 dc in next ch-2 sp, ch 1,
holding Squares with **wrong** sides together, slip st
in corner sp on **adjacent Square**, ch 1, 3 dc in
same ch-2 sp on **new Square**, ch 1, slip st in next
ch-1 sp on **adjacent Square**, 3 dc in next ch-2 sp
on **new Square**, ch 1, (slip st in next corner sp on
adjacent Square, ch 1) twice, 3 dc in same
ch-2 sp on **new Square**, ch 1, slip st in next
ch-1 sp on **adjacent Square**, 3 dc in next ch-2 sp
on **new Square**, ch 1, slip st in next corner sp on
adjacent Square, ch 1, 3 dc in same ch-2 sp on
new Square, ch 1; join with slip st to first dc,
finish off.

Design by Judy Bolin.

PLACEMENT DIAGRAM

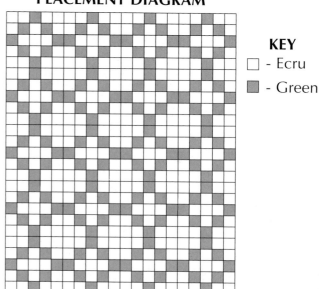

KEY
☐ - Ecru
▦ - Green

A SIMPLE ARRANGEMENT OF SMALL SQUARES DELIVERS A TASTE OF COUNTRY TO THIS CUDDLY BLANKET. THE BLOCKS CAN BE WHIPPED UP IN ANY COLOR COMBINATION TO COMPLEMENT YOUR FAVORITE LOUNGING SPOT.

Finished Size: 47" x 65"

MATERIALS

Worsted Weight Yarn:
Lt Green - 31 ounces,
(880 grams, 2,020 yards)
Blue - 20 ounces, (570 grams, 1,305 yards)
Ecru - 14 ounces, (400 grams, 910 yards)
Crochet hook, size H (5.00 mm) **or** size needed for gauge
Yarn needle

GAUGE: Each Strip = 4¼" wide

Gauge Swatch: 1½"w x 9"h
Foundation Row (Right side)**:** With Blue, ch 4, work Beginning Popcorn, ch 3, dc in third ch from hook to form a ring, ch 4, work Beginning Popcorn, ★ ch 6, work Beginning Popcorn, ch 3, dc in third ch from hook to form a ring, ch 4, work Beginning Popcorn; repeat from ★ once **more**: 6 Beginning Popcorns.
Rnd 1: Work same as Strip.

STITCH GUIDE

TREBLE CROCHET (abbreviated tr)
YO twice, insert hook in st or sp indicated, YO and pull up a loop (4 loops on hook), (YO and draw through 2 loops on hook) 3 times.

BEGINNING POPCORN
3 Dc in fourth ch from hook **(3 skipped chs count as first dc)**, drop loop from hook, insert hook in first dc of 4-dc group, hook dropped loop and draw through.

POPCORN
4 Dc in sp indicated, drop loop from hook, insert hook in first dc of 4-dc group, hook dropped loop and draw through.

FRONT POST DOUBLE CROCHET
    (abbreviated FPdc)
YO, insert hook from **front** to **back** around post of st indicated **(Fig. 4, page 143)**, YO and pull up a loop (3 loops on hook), (YO and draw through 2 loops on hook) twice.

FRONT POST TREBLE CROCHET
    (abbreviated FPtr)
YO twice, insert hook from **front** to **back** around post of st indicated **(Fig. 4, page 143)**, YO and pull up a loop (4 loops on hook), (YO and draw through 2 loops on hook) 3 times.

FRONT POST DOUBLE CROCHET CLUSTER
    (abbreviated FPdc Cluster) (uses next 2 sc)
★ YO, insert hook from **front** to **back** around post of **next** sc on Rnd 1 **(Fig. 4, page 143)**, YO and pull up a loop, YO and draw through 2 loops on hook; repeat from ★ once **more**, YO and draw through all 3 loops on hook.

STRIP (Make 11)

Foundation Row (Right side)**:** With Blue, ch 4, work Beginning Popcorn, ch 3, dc in third ch from hook to form a ring, ch 4, work Beginning Popcorn, ★ ch 6, work Beginning Popcorn, ch 3, dc in third ch from hook to form a ring, ch 4, work Beginning Popcorn; repeat from ★ 17 times **more**: 38 Popcorns and 19 rings.

Note: Loop a short piece of yarn around any stitch to mark Foundation Row as **right** side.

Rnd 1: Working across dc side of rings, ch 4, skip first Popcorn, † work (Popcorn, ch 3, Popcorn) in next ring, ch 4, ★ skip next Popcorn, sc in next ch, ch 1, sc in next ch, ch 4, skip next Popcorn, work (Popcorn, ch 3, Popcorn) in next ring, ch 4; repeat from ★ across to last Popcorn †; working in free loops of Foundation ch **(Fig. 3b, page 143)** and in ch-3 side of rings, slip st in ch at base of last Popcorn, ch 4, repeat from † to † once; join with slip st to st at base of beginning ch-4, finish off: 76 Popcorns and 150 sps.

Rnd 2: With **right** side facing, join Lt Green with slip st in first ch-4 sp; ch 4 **(counts as first tr)**, (2 tr, 3 dc) in same sp, † 4 dc in each of next 2 sps, skip next sc, working **behind** next ch-1 **(Fig. 6, page 143)**, tr around Foundation ch, ★ 4 dc in each of next 3 sps, skip next sc, working **behind** next ch-1, tr around Foundation ch; repeat

Continued on page 36.

THE REFRESHING IMAGE OF ABUNDANT
BLUEBERRIES GIVES THIS LUSCIOUS AFGHAN
A TRANQUIL TWIST. POPCORN STITCHES
CREATE THE BLUEBERRY CLUSTERS, AND
THE ROUNDED ENDS OF THE STRIPS FORM
A NATURAL SCALLOPED EDGE.

Finished Size: 52" x 70"

MATERIALS
Worsted Weight Yarn:
 Green - 43 ounces,
  (1,220 grams, 2,735 yards)
 Pink - 16 ounces, (450 grams, 1,020 yards)
 Dk Pink - 4 ounces, (110 grams, 255 yards)
 Crochet hook, size G (4.00 mm) **or** size needed
  for gauge

GAUGE SWATCH: 6" (straight edge to straight edge)
Work same as First Motif.

STITCH GUIDE

DECREASE (uses next 2 dc)
★ YO, insert hook in **next** dc, YO and pull up
a loop, YO and draw through 2 loops on hook;
repeat from ★ once **more**, YO and draw
through all 3 loops on hook (**counts as one
dc**).

BEGINNING CLUSTER (uses next 4 dc)
Ch 2, ★ YO, insert hook in **next** dc, YO and
pull up a loop, YO and draw through 2 loops
on hook; repeat from ★ 3 times **more**, YO and
draw through all 5 loops on hook.

CLUSTER (uses next 5 dc)
★ YO, insert hook in **next** dc, YO and pull up
a loop, YO and draw through 2 loops on hook;
repeat from ★ 4 times **more**, YO and draw
through all 6 loops on hook.

FIRST MOTIF
With Dk Pink, ch 6; join with slip st to form a ring.

Rnd 1 (Right side)**:** Ch 1, 12 sc in ring; join with
slip st to first sc.

Note: Loop a short piece of yarn around any stitch
to mark Rnd 1 as **right** side.

Rnd 2: Ch 1, sc in same st, ch 4, skip next sc, ★ sc
in next sc, ch 4, skip next sc; repeat from ★
around; join with slip st to first sc, finish off:
6 ch-4 sps.

Rnd 3: With **right** side facing, join Pink with slip st
in any sc; ch 1, sc in same st, ch 4, (sc in next sc,
ch 4) around; join with slip st to first sc.

Rnd 4: Working in ch-4 sps on Rnd 2 and in **front**
of ch-4 sps on Rnd 3 (*Fig. 6, page 143*), slip st in
first ch-4 sp, ch 3, [dc, (ch 1, dc) 6 times, ch 3,
slip st] in same sp, [slip st, ch 3, dc, (ch 1, dc) 6
times, ch 3, slip st] in next ch-4 sp and in each
ch-4 sp around; join with slip st to first slip st,
finish off: 6 petals.

Rnd 5: With **right** side facing and working in
ch-4 sps on Rnd 3, join Green with slip st in any
ch-4 sp; ch 3 (**counts as first dc, now and
throughout**), 4 dc in same sp, ch 2, (5 dc in next
ch-4 sp, ch 2) around; join with slip st to first dc:
30 dc.

Rnd 6: Ch 3, dc in same st, dc in next 3 dc, 2 dc
in next dc, ch 5, ★ 2 dc in next dc, dc in next
3 dc, 2 dc in next dc, ch 5; repeat from ★ around;
join with slip st to first dc: 42 dc and 6 ch-5 sps.

Rnd 7: Ch 2, dc in next 4 dc, decrease, ch 3, (dc,
ch 1, dc) in next ch-5 sp, ch 3, ★ decrease, dc in
next 3 dc, decrease, ch 3, (dc, ch 1, dc) in next
ch-5 sp, ch 3; repeat from ★ around; join with
slip st to first dc: 42 dc and 18 sps.

Rnd 8: Work Beginning Cluster, ch 3, dc in next
ch-3 sp and in next dc, (dc, ch 3, dc) in next
ch-1 sp, dc in next dc and in next ch-3 sp, ch 3,
★ work Cluster, ch 3, dc in next ch-3 sp and in
next dc, (dc, ch 3, dc) in next ch-1 sp, dc in next
dc and in next ch-3 sp, ch 3; repeat from ★
around; join with slip st to top of Beginning
Cluster, finish off.

ADDITIONAL MOTIFS
The method used to connect the Motifs is a
no-sew joining also known as "join-as-you-go".
After the First Motif is made, each remaining Motif
is worked through Rnd 7, then crocheted together
as Rnd 8 is worked.

Work same as First Motif through Rnd 7; do **not**
finish off: 42 dc and 18 sps.

Continued on page 37.

PRETTY PINK BLOOMS SPRING FROM A FIELD OF SOFT GREEN TO MAKE THIS DELICATE AFGHAN. HEXAGONS FEATURING THREE-DIMENSIONAL PETALS FORM A HONEYCOMB EFFECT.

Finished Size: 46" x 59"

MATERIALS

Worsted Weight Yarn:
  Gold - 21³/₄ ounces, (620 grams, 1,490 yards)
  Brown - 17 ounces, (480 grams, 1,165 yards)
  Green - 15¹/₂ ounces,
    (440 grams, 1,065 yards)
  Blue - 6³/₄ ounces, (190 grams, 465 yards)
  Crochet hook, size G (4.00 mm) **or** size needed
  for gauge

GAUGE: Each Motif = 7¹/₂"
        (straight edge to straight edge)

Gauge Swatch: 2⁵/₈" diameter
Work same as Motif through Rnd 2.
Finish off.

STITCH GUIDE

TREBLE CROCHET (abbreviated tr)
YO twice, insert hook in sp indicated, YO and
pull up a loop (4 loops on hook), (YO and
draw through 2 loops on hook) 3 times.

BEGINNING POPCORN
Ch 3 **(counts as first dc)**, 2 dc in st or sp
indicated, drop loop from hook, insert hook in
first dc of 3-dc group, hook dropped loop and
pull through.

POPCORN
3 Dc in st or sp indicated, drop loop from
hook, insert hook in first dc of 3-dc group,
hook dropped loop and pull through.

PICOT
Ch 3, slip st in top of st just made **(Fig. 7,
page 143)**.

PETAL
Ch 3, ★ YO twice, insert hook in st or sp
indicated, YO and pull up a loop, (YO and
draw through 2 loops on hook) twice; repeat
from ★ once **more**, YO and draw through all
3 loops on hook, work Picot, ch 3.

**FRONT POST DOUBLE CROCHET
    (abbreviated FPdc)**
YO, insert hook from **front** to **back** around
post of st indicated **(Fig. 4, page 143)**, YO and
pull up a loop, (YO and draw through 2 loops
on hook) twice. Skip st behind FPdc.

SLIP ST JOINING
With **right** side of two Motifs facing you and
matching sts, beginning with slip knot on hook
and keeping yarn to **back** of work, insert hook
from top to bottom in Back Loop Only of first
st on first Motif and from top to bottom in
Back Loop Only of first st on Second Motif
(Fig. 1), YO and draw through all 3 loops on
hook, ★ insert hook from top to bottom in
Back Loop Only of next st on first Motif and
from top to bottom in Back Loop Only of next
st on second Motif, YO and draw through all
3 loops on hook; repeat from ★ across.

Fig. 1

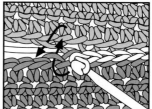

MOTIF (Make 50)

With Brown, ch 4; join with slip st to form a ring.

Rnd 1 (Right side): Work Beginning Popcorn in
ring, ch 2, (work Popcorn in ring, ch 2) 5 times;
join with slip st to top of Beginning Popcorn:
6 Popcorns and 6 ch-2 sps.

Note: Loop a short piece of yarn around any stitch
to mark Rnd 1 as **right** side.

Rnd 2: Slip st in first ch-2 sp, work (Beginning
Popcorn, ch 2, Popcorn) in same sp, ch 2, (work
Popcorn, ch 2) twice in each ch-2 sp around; join
with slip st to top of Beginning Popcorn, do **not**
finish off: 12 Popcorns and 12 ch-2 sps.

Continued on page 38.

THE SUNFLOWERS ON THIS BLANKET ARE ALIVE WITH SUMMER SPLENDOR. EACH HEXAGONAL BLOSSOM HAS A LUSH POPCORN STITCH CENTER AND FRILLY PETALS.

Finished Size: 53" x 77"

MATERIALS
Worsted Weight Yarn:
   Rose - 24 ounces, (680 grams, 1,580 yards)
   Yellow - 15 ounces, (430 grams, 985 yards)
   Green - 9 ounces, (260 grams, 595 yards)
   Lt Rose - 7 ounces, (200 grams, 460 yards)
Crochet hook, size I (5.50 mm) **or** size needed
   for gauge
Yarn needle

GAUGE: Large Square = 8"

Gauge Swatch: 4" square
Work same as Small Square.

LARGE SQUARE (Make 24)
A marker is used to help distinguish the beginning of each round being worked. Place a 2" scrap piece of yarn before the first stitch of each round, moving marker after each round is complete.

Rnd 1 (Right side): With Yellow, ch 2, 6 sc in second ch from hook; do **not** join, place marker.

Note: Loop a short piece of yarn around any stitch to mark Rnd 1 as **right** side.

Rnds 2 and 3: 2 Sc in Back Loop Only of each sc around *(Fig. 2, page 143)*: 24 sc.

Rnd 4: Working in Back Loops Only, ★ sc in next sc, ch 1, skip next sc, hdc in next sc, (dc, ch 3, dc) in next sc, hdc in next sc, ch 1, skip next sc; repeat from ★ around; join with slip st to **both** loops of next sc, remove marker: 12 sps.

Rnd 5: Working in both loops, ch 3 (**counts as first dc, now and throughout**), 2 dc in same st, ch 1, (3 dc, ch 3, 3 dc) in next ch-3 sp, ch 1, ★ 3 dc in next sc, ch 1, (3 dc, ch 3, 3 dc) in next ch-3 sp, ch 1; repeat from ★ around; join with slip st to first dc, finish off.

Rnd 6: With **right** side facing and working in free loops on Rnds 1-3 *(Fig. 3a, page 143)*, join Rose with slip st in first sc on Rnd 1; ch 2, dc in same st, ch 2 (**Petal made**), [(slip st, ch 2, dc) in next sc, ch 2] 19 times, place marker around last slip st worked for joining placement, ★ skip next sc,

(slip st, ch 2, dc) in next sc, ch 2; repeat from ★ 10 times **more**; join with slip st to marked slip st, finish off: 31 Petals.

Rnd 7: With **right** side facing, join Green with slip st in any ch-3 sp on Rnd 5; ch 3, (2 dc, ch 3, 3 dc) in same sp, ch 1, (3 dc in next ch-1 sp, ch 1) across to next ch-3 sp, ★ (3 dc, ch 3, 3 dc) in ch-3 sp, ch 1, (3 dc in next ch-1 sp, ch 1) across to next ch-3 sp; repeat from ★ around; join with slip st to first dc, finish off: 16 sps.

Rnd 8: With Lt Rose, repeat Rnd 7: 20 sps.

Rnd 9: With Yellow, repeat Rnd 7: 24 sps.

Rnd 10: With Rose, repeat Rnd 7: 28 sps.

SMALL SQUARE
Make 151 in the following color sequence:

	Square A	Square B
Make	116	35
Rnd 1	Yellow	Lt Rose
Rnd 2	Green	Yellow
Rnd 3	Rose	Rose

Rnd 1 (Right side): With first color, ch 4, 2 dc in fourth ch from hook, ch 3, (3 dc in same st, ch 3) 3 times; join with slip st to top of beginning ch, finish off: 4 ch-3 sps.

Note: Mark Rnd 1 as **right** side.

Rnd 2: With **right** side facing, join next color with slip st in any ch-3 sp; ch 3, (2 dc, ch 3, 3 dc) in same sp, ch 1, ★ (3 dc, ch 3, 3 dc) in next ch-3 sp, ch 1; repeat from ★ around; join with slip st to first dc, finish off: 8 sps.

Rnd 3: With **right** side facing, join Rose with slip st in any ch-3 sp; ch 3, (2 dc, ch 3, 3 dc) in same sp, ch 1, 3 dc in next ch-1 sp, ch 1, ★ (3 dc, ch 3, 3 dc) in next ch-3 sp, ch 1, 3 dc in next ch-1 sp, ch 1; repeat from ★ around; join with slip st to first dc, finish off: 12 sps.

Continued on page 39.

B URSTING WITH RICH HUES, OUR EYE-
CATCHING FLORAL THROW WOULD MAKE A
LOVELY GIFT FOR A GARDENING ENTHUSIAST.
AMAZINGLY LIFELIKE, THE DENSE PETALS
REACH OUT FOR ATTENTION.

Rich Blossoms

Finished Size: 49" x 60"

MATERIALS

Worsted Weight Yarn:
- Dk Green - 19 ounces,
  (540 grams, 1,305 yards)
- Ecru - 13 ounces, (370 grams, 890 yards)
- Green - 11½ ounces, (330 grams, 790 yards)
- Dk Blue - 1¾ ounces, (50 grams, 120 yards)
- Blue - 1½ ounces, (40 grams, 105 yards)
- Purple - 1¼ ounces, (35 grams, 85 yards)
- Dk Pink - ¾ ounce, (20 grams, 50 yards)
- Dk Purple - ½ ounce, (15 grams, 35 yards)
- Pink - ¼ ounce, (10 grams, 15 yards)

Crochet hook, size H (5.00 mm) **or** size needed for gauge

Yarn needle

GAUGE SWATCH: 5¾" (point to point)
Work same as Triangle.

STITCH GUIDE

BEGINNING DC CLUSTER
Ch 3, ★ YO, insert hook in sp indicated, YO and pull up a loop, YO and draw through 2 loops on hook; repeat from ★ once **more**, YO and draw through all 3 loops on hook.

DC CLUSTER
★ YO, insert hook in sp indicated, YO and pull up a loop, YO and draw through 2 loops on hook; repeat from ★ 2 times **more**, YO and draw through all 4 loops on hook.

TR CLUSTER
★ YO twice, insert hook in sp indicated, YO and pull up a loop, (YO and draw through 2 loops on hook) twice; repeat from ★ 2 times **more**, YO and draw through all 4 loops on hook.

PICOT
Ch 4, slip st in fourth ch from hook (**counts as one ch-4 sp**).

DECREASE (uses next 2 ch-3 sps)
★ YO twice, insert hook in **next** ch-3 sp, YO and pull up a loop, (YO and draw through 2 loops on hook) twice; repeat from ★ once **more**, YO and draw through all 3 loops on hook (**counts as one tr**).

TRIANGLE (Make 130)

The color used on Rnd 1 of each Triangle will vary. Make the number of Triangles indicated for **each** of the following colors: Dk Blue - 40, Blue - 32, Purple - 28, Dk Pink - 16, Dk Purple - 12, and Pink - 2.

Ch 5; join with slip st to form a ring.

Rnd 1 (Right side): Work Beginning dc Cluster in ring, ch 3, work dc Cluster in ring, ch 5, ★ work dc Cluster in ring, ch 3, work dc Cluster in ring, ch 5; repeat from ★ once **more**; join with slip st to top of Beginning dc Cluster, finish off: 6 sps.

Note: Loop a short piece of yarn around any stitch to mark Rnd 1 as **right** side.

Rnd 2: With **right** side facing, join Green with slip st in any ch-5 sp; in same sp work (Beginning dc Cluster, ch 4, tr Cluster, Picot, ch 4, dc Cluster), ch 3, sc in next ch-3 sp, ch 3, ★ in next ch-5 sp work (dc Cluster, ch 4, tr Cluster, Picot, ch 4, dc Cluster), ch 3, sc in next ch-3 sp, ch 3; repeat from ★ once **more**; join with slip st to top of Beginning dc Cluster, finish off: 12 sts and 15 sps.

Rnd 3: With **right** side facing, join Dk Green with slip st in any Picot (ch-4 sp); ch 3 (**counts as first dc, now and throughout**), (2 dc, ch 3, 3 dc) in same sp, ★ † 4 dc in next ch-4 sp, dc in next dc Cluster, (3 dc in next ch-3 sp, dc in next st) twice, 4 dc in next ch-4 sp †, (3 dc, ch 3, 3 dc) in next Picot; repeat from ★ once **more**, then repeat from † to † once; join with slip st to first dc, finish off: 69 dc and 3 ch-3 sps.

Rnd 4: With **right** side facing, join Ecru with slip st in any ch-3 sp; ch 1, (sc, ch 3, sc) in same sp, sc in next dc, (ch 1, skip next dc, sc in next dc) across to next ch-3 sp, ★ (sc, ch 3, sc) in ch-3 sp, sc in next dc, (ch 1, skip next dc, sc in next dc) across to next ch-3 sp; repeat from ★ once **more**; join with slip st to first sc, finish off: 42 sc.

Continued on page 40.

BLOOMING WITH RICH COLORS, THE
PRETTY TRIANGLE-SHAPED MOTIFS ON THIS
WRAP CREATE AN INTRICATE GARDEN. A HELPFUL
DIAGRAM MAKES IT EASY TO ARRANGE THE
MOTIFS IN AN ARTFUL MANNER.

Finished Size: 55" x 65¹/₂"

MATERIALS

Worsted Weight Yarn:
   White - 24 ounces, (680 grams, 1,565 yards)
   Lt Green - 15 ounces,
      (430 grams, 980 yards)
   Yellow - 9 ounces, (260 grams, 585 yards)
Crochet hooks, sizes F (3.75 mm) **and** G
   (4.00 mm) **or** sizes needed for gauge
Yarn needle

GAUGE: Each Strip through Border = 7" wide

Gauge Swatch: 4¹/₂" diameter
Work same as First Flower.

STITCH GUIDE

DOUBLE CROCHET CLUSTER
   (abbreviated dc Cluster)
YO, insert hook in same sp, YO and pull up a loop, YO and draw through 2 loops on hook, for second leg, YO, insert hook in ch-3 sp at tip of next petal, YO and pull up a loop, YO and draw through 2 loops on hook, YO and draw through all 3 loops on hook.

CLUSTER
YO twice, insert hook in same sp, YO and pull up a loop, (YO and draw through 2 loops on hook) twice, YO, insert hook in sp at tip of next petal on same Flower, YO and pull up a loop, YO and draw through 2 loops on hook, YO, insert hook in sp at tip of next petal on next Flower, YO and pull up a loop, YO and draw through 2 loops on hook, YO twice, insert hook in sp at tip of next petal on same Flower, YO and pull up a loop, (YO and draw through 2 loops on hook) twice, YO and draw through all 5 loops on hook.

FRONT POST SINGLE CROCHET
   (abbreviated FPsc)
Insert hook from **front** to **back** around post of dc indicated *(Fig. 4, page 143)*, YO and pull up a loop, YO and draw through both loops on hook.

SHORT PETAL
Ch 8 **loosely**; working in back ridge of chs *(Fig. 1, page 143)*, sc in fourth ch from hook, dc in next 2 chs, hdc in next ch, sc in last ch.

LONG PETAL
Ch 9 **loosely**; working in back ridge of chs *(Fig. 1, page 143)*, sc in fourth ch from hook, hdc in next ch, dc in next 2 chs, hdc in next ch, sc in last ch.

SHELL
(2 Dc, ch 1, 2 dc) in st indicated.

DECREASE
Pull up a loop in next 3 sts, YO and draw through all 4 loops on hook.

FIRST STRIP
FIRST FLOWER
With larger size hook and Yellow, ch 4; join with slip st to form a ring.

Rnd 1 (Right side): Ch 3 **(counts as first dc, now and throughout)**, 11 dc in ring; join with slip st to first dc, finish off: 12 dc.

Note: Loop a short piece of yarn around any stitch to mark Rnd 1 as **right** side.

Rnd 2: With **right** side facing, join White with slip st in any dc; work Short Petal, work FPsc around same dc as slip st, ★ (slip st in next dc, work Long Petal, work FPsc around same dc as slip st) twice, slip st in next dc, work Short Petal, work FPsc around same dc as slip st; repeat from ★ once **more**, place marker around 3 skipped chs at tip of fifth Petal made for joining placement, (slip st in next dc, work Long Petal, work FPsc around same dc as slip st) 5 times; join with slip st to slip st at base of first Petal, finish off: 12 Petals.

NEXT 12 FLOWERS
With larger size hook and Yellow, ch 4; join with slip st to form a ring.

Rnd 1 (Right side): Ch 3, 11 dc in ring; join with slip st to first dc, finish off: 12 dc.

Note: Mark Rnd 1 as **right** side.

Continued on page 40.

Pink Carnations

Finished Size: 43" x 59"

MATERIALS

Worsted Weight Yarn:
Ecru - 17½ ounces, (500 grams, 1,200 yards)
Lt Green - 15½ ounces,
   (440 grams, 1,065 yards)
Pink - 10½ ounces, (300 grams, 720 yards)
Green - 6 ounces, (170 grams, 410 yards)
Crochet hook, size I (5.50 mm) **or** size needed
   for gauge
Yarn needle

GAUGE: Each Square = 8¼"

Gauge Swatch: 4"
Work same as Square through Rnd 5.

STITCH GUIDE

TREBLE CROCHET (abbreviated tr)
YO twice, insert hook in sp indicated, YO and
pull up a loop (4 loops on hook), (YO and
draw through 2 loops on hook) 3 times.

BEGINNING CLUSTER
Ch 2, ★ YO, insert hook in sp indicated, YO
and pull up a loop, YO and draw through
2 loops on hook; repeat from ★ 3 times **more**,
YO and draw through all 5 loops on hook.

CLUSTER
★ YO, insert hook in sp indicated, YO and pull
up a loop, YO and draw through 2 loops on
hook; repeat from ★ 4 times **more**, YO and
draw through all 6 loops on hook.

POPCORN
4 Dc in sp indicated, drop loop from hook,
insert hook in first dc of 4-dc group, hook
dropped loop and draw through.

PICOT
Ch 1, sc in top of sc just made **(Fig. 7,
page 143)**.

PANEL (Make 3)
SQUARE (Make 21)
Each Panel consists of 7 Squares.

With Pink, ch 6; join with slip st to form a ring.

Rnd 1 (Right side): Ch 1, (sc in ring, ch 3) 8 times;
join with slip st to first sc: 8 ch-3 sps.

Note: Loop a short piece of yarn around any stitch
to mark Rnd 1 as **right** side.

Rnd 2: Ch 1, sc in same st, ch 5, (sc in next sc,
ch 5) around; join with slip st to first sc:
8 ch-5 sps.

Rnd 3: Working in ch-3 sps on Rnd 1 and keeping
ch-5 to back of work, slip st in first ch-3 sp, ch 1,
[sc, ch 1, (dc, ch 1) 5 times, sc] in same sp and in
each ch-3 sp around; join with slip st to first sc.

Rnd 4: Ch 1, sc in same st, ch 2, (sc in next dc,
ch 2) 5 times, ★ (sc in next sc, ch 2) twice, (sc in
next dc, ch 2) 5 times; repeat from ★ around to
last sc, sc in last sc, ch 2; join with slip st to first
sc, finish off.

Rnd 5: With **right** side facing, join Lt Green with
slip st in any ch-5 sp on Rnd 2; ch 3 **(counts as
first dc, now and throughout)**, 2 dc in same sp,
(3 tr, ch 2, 3 tr) in next ch-5 sp, ★ 3 dc in next
ch-5 sp, (3 tr, ch 2, 3 tr) in next ch-5 sp; repeat
from ★ 2 times **more**; join with slip st to first dc,
finish off: 36 sts and 4 ch-2 sps.

Rnd 6: With **right** side facing, join Ecru with slip st
in any ch-2 sp; ch 5 **(counts as first dc plus ch 2,
now and throughout)**, 2 dc in same sp, dc in each
st across to next ch-2 sp, ★ (2 dc, ch 2, 2 dc) in
ch-2 sp, dc in each st across to next ch-2 sp;
repeat from ★ 2 times **more**, dc in same sp as first
dc; join with slip st to first dc: 52 dc.

Rnd 7: Slip st in first ch-2 sp, ch 5, 2 dc in same
sp, dc in each dc across to next ch-2 sp, ★ (2 dc,
ch 2, 2 dc) in ch-2 sp, dc in each dc across to
next ch-2 sp; repeat from ★ 2 times **more**, dc in
same sp as first dc; join with slip st to first dc,
finish off: 68 dc.

Continued on page 42.

THREE-DIMENSIONAL DESIGNS ARE THE
KEY TO THIS GORGEOUS THROW. JOIN
SQUARES INTO PANELS AND THEN CONNECT
THEM WITH STRIPS OF CLUSTERS FOR
A UNIQUELY DECORATIVE PIECE.

Garden Patchwork

Finished Size: 41" x 58"

MATERIALS
Worsted Weight Yarn:
   Off-White - 20 ounces,
      (570 grams, 1,165 yards)
   Green - 16 ounces, (450 grams, 935 yards)
   Scraps - 15 ounces,
      (430 grams, 875 yards) **total**
   Note: We used 6 different scrap colors.
      Each Square A requires 5¾ yards.
Crochet hook, size G (4.00 mm) **or** size needed
   for gauge

GAUGE SWATCH: 3¼" square
Work same as First Square.

STITCH GUIDE

> **BEGINNING CLUSTER**
> ★ YO twice, insert hook in st indicated, YO
> and pull up a loop, (YO and draw through
> 2 loops on hook) twice; repeat from ★ once
> **more**, YO and draw through all 3 loops on
> hook.
>
> **CLUSTER**
> ★ YO twice, insert hook in sc indicated, YO
> and pull up a loop, (YO and draw through
> 2 loops on hook) twice; repeat from ★ 2 times
> **more**, YO and draw through all 4 loops on
> hook.

Following Placement Diagram, page 43, make
Squares indicated.

SQUARE A
FIRST SQUARE
With color desired, ch 5; join with slip st to form a
ring.

Rnd 1 (Right side)**:** Ch 1, 8 sc in ring; join with
slip st to first sc.

Note: Loop a short piece of yarn around any stitch
to mark Rnd 1 as **right** side.

Rnd 2: Ch 3, work Beginning Cluster in same st,
ch 4, (work Cluster in next sc, ch 4) around; join
with slip st to top of Beginning Cluster, finish off:
8 Clusters.

Rnd 3: With **right** side facing, join Green with
slip st in any ch-4 sp; ch 3 **(counts as first dc, now
and throughout)**, (2 dc, ch 2, 3 dc) in same sp,
ch 1, 3 dc in next ch-4 sp, ch 1, ★ (3 dc, ch 2,
3 dc) in next ch-4 sp, ch 1, 3 dc in next ch-4 sp,
ch 1; repeat from ★ around; join with slip st to
first dc, finish off: 12 3-dc groups.

ADDITIONAL SQUARES
The method used to connect the Squares is a
no-sew joining also known as "join-as-you-go".
After the First Square is made, each remaining
Square is worked through Rnd 2, then crocheted
together as Rnd 3 is worked.

Work same as First Square through Rnd 2:
8 Clusters.

Rnd 3 (Joining rnd)**:** With **right** side facing, join
Green with slip st in any ch-4 sp; complete by
working One or Two Side Joining *(Fig. 10,
page 144)*.

SQUARE B
With Off-White, ch 4; join with slip st to form a
ring.

Rnd 1 (Right side)**:** Ch 3, 2 dc in ring, (ch 2, 3 dc
in ring) 3 times, ch 1, sc in first dc to form last
ch-2 sp: 4 ch-2 sps.

Rnd 2: Ch 3, 2 dc in same sp, ch 1, ★ (3 dc, ch 2,
3 dc) in next ch-2 sp, ch 1; repeat from ★ 2 times
more, 3 dc in same sp as first dc, ch 1, sc in first
dc to form last ch-2 sp; do **not** finish off: 8 sps.

Rnd 3 (Joining rnd)**:** Work One or Two Side
Joining.

Continued on page 43.

Finished Size: 45½" x 62"

MATERIALS

Worsted Weight Yarn:
   White - 21 ounces, (600 grams, 1,370 yards)
   Pink - 18 ounces, (510 grams, 1,175 yards)
   Green - 7 ounces, (200 grams, 455 yards)
Crochet hook, size H (5.00 mm) **or** size needed
   for gauge

GAUGE: Each Flower = 4¼" diameter
         Each Strip = 6½" wide

Gauge Swatch: 3½" diameter
Work same as First Flower through Rnd 2.

STITCH GUIDE

TREBLE CROCHET (abbreviated tr)
YO twice, insert hook in st indicated, YO and
pull up a loop (4 loops on hook), (YO and
draw through 2 loops on hook) 3 times.

DECREASE
YO, insert hook in next sc on same Flower, YO
and pull up a loop, YO and draw through
2 loops on hook, YO, insert hook in next
joining, YO and pull up a loop, YO and draw
through 2 loops on hook, YO, insert hook in
next sc on next Flower, YO and pull up a loop,
YO and draw through 2 loops on hook, YO
and draw through all 4 loops on hook.

FIRST STRIP
FIRST FLOWER

Rnd 1 (Right side)**:** With White, ch 4, 15 dc in
fourth ch from hook (**3 skipped chs count as first
dc**); join with slip st to first dc, finish off: 16 dc.

Note: Loop a short piece of yarn around any stitch
to mark Rnd 1 as **right** side.

Rnd 2: With **right** side facing, join Pink with sc in
any dc **(see Joining With Sc, page 142)**; sc in next
3 dc, ch 5, **turn**; skip first 3 sc, slip st in next sc,
ch 1, **turn**; 11 sc in ch-5 sp, slip st in side of next
sc (petal made), ★ sc in next 2 dc, ch 5, **turn**;

working in **front** of petal just made, slip st in
second skipped sc, ch 1, **turn**; 11 sc in ch-5 sp,
slip st in side of next sc; repeat from ★ 5 times
more; join with slip st to first sc, working in **front**
of first petal, slip st in next sc, ch 5, **turn**; working
in **front** of last petal made, slip st in second
skipped sc, ch 1, **turn**; 11 sc in ch-5 sp, slip st in
same st as ch-5; finish off: 8 petals.

Rnd 3: With **right** side facing and working in Back
Loops Only **(Fig. 2, page 143)**, join Green with sc
in center sc of any petal; ch 1, skipping next 2 sc
on same petal and first 2 sc on next petal and
working in **both** petals **(Fig. 1)**, (dc, ch 3, dc) in
next sc, ch 1, ★ skip next 2 sc on new petal, sc in
next sc, ch 1, skipping next 2 sc on same petal
and first 2 sc on next petal and working in **both**
petals, (dc, ch 3, dc) in next sc, ch 1; repeat from
★ around, place marker around last ch-3 made for
joining placement; join with slip st to **both** loops
of first sc, finish off: 8 sc and 8 ch-3 sps.

Fig. 1

REMAINING 13 FLOWERS
Work same as First Flower through Rnd 2:
8 petals.

Rnd 3 (Joining rnd)**:** With **right** side facing and
working in Back Loops Only, join Green with sc in
center sc of any petal; ch 1, ★ skipping next 2 sc
on same petal and first 2 sc on next petal and
working in **both** petals, (dc, ch 3, dc) in next sc,
ch 1, skip next 2 sc on new petal, sc in next sc,
ch 1; repeat from ★ 5 times **more**, place marker
around fourth ch-3 made for joining placement,

Continued on page 44.

Quiet Moment

Finished Size: 51" x 71"

MATERIALS
Worsted Weight Yarn:
42 ounces, (1,190 grams, 2,880 yards)
Crochet hook, size H (5.00 mm) **or** size needed for gauge
Yarn needle

GAUGE: Each Motif = 6³/₄"
(straight edge to straight edge)

Gauge Swatch: 3¹/₂" diameter
Work same as Motif through Rnd 2.

STITCH GUIDE

TREBLE CROCHET (abbreviated tr)
YO twice, insert hook in st or sp indicated, YO and pull up a loop (4 loops on hook), (YO and draw through 2 loops on hook) 3 times.

BEGINNING CLUSTER (uses next 3 tr)
Ch 3, ★ YO twice, insert hook in **next** tr, YO and pull up a loop, (YO and draw through 2 loops on hook) twice; repeat from ★ 2 times **more**, YO and draw through all 4 loops on hook.

CLUSTER (uses next 4 tr)
★ YO twice, insert hook in **next** tr, YO and pull up a loop, (YO and draw through 2 loops on hook) twice; repeat from ★ 3 times **more**, YO and draw through all 5 loops on hook.

DECREASE (uses next 3 dc)
† YO, insert hook in **next** dc, YO and pull up a loop, YO and draw through 2 loops on hook †, skip next dc, repeat from † to † once, YO and draw through all 3 loops on hook **(counts as one dc).**

3-DC DECREASE (uses next 3 ch-1 sps)
★ YO, insert hook in **next** ch-1 sp, YO and pull up a loop, YO and draw through 2 loops on hook; repeat from ★ 2 times **more**, YO and draw through all 4 loops on hook **(counts as one dc).**

MOTIF (Make 72)

Rnd 1 (Right side)**:** Ch 6, (dc, ch 2) 5 times in sixth ch from hook; join with slip st to fourth ch of beginning ch-6: 6 ch-2 sps.

Note: Loop a short piece of yarn around any stitch to mark Rnd 1 as **right** side.

Rnd 2: Slip st in first ch-2 sp, ch 4 **(counts as first tr, now and throughout)**, 3 tr in same sp, ch 3, (4 tr in next ch-2 sp, ch 3) around; join with slip st to first tr: 24 tr and 6 ch-3 sps.

Rnd 3: Work Beginning Cluster, ch 2, (tr, ch 3, tr) in next ch-3 sp, ch 2, ★ work Cluster, ch 2, (tr, ch 3, tr) in next ch-3 sp, ch 2; repeat from ★ around; join with slip st to top of Beginning Cluster: 18 sts and 18 sps.

Rnd 4: Ch 4, 2 tr in next ch-2 sp, tr in next tr, (2 tr, ch 3, 2 tr) in next ch-3 sp, tr in next tr, 2 tr in next ch-2 sp, ★ tr in next Cluster, 2 tr in next ch-2 sp, tr in next tr, (2 tr, ch 3, 2 tr) in next ch-3 sp, tr in next tr, 2 tr in next ch-2 sp; repeat from ★ around; join with slip st to first tr, finish off: 66 tr and 6 ch-3 sps.

HALF MOTIF (Make 10)

Ch 4; join with slip st to form a ring.

Row 1: Ch 5 **(counts as first dc plus ch 2)**, dc in ring, (ch 2, dc in ring) twice: 4 dc and 3 ch-2 sps.

Row 2 (Right side)**:** Ch 5 **(counts as first tr plus ch 1, now and throughout)**, turn; 4 tr in next ch-2 sp, (ch 3, 4 tr in next ch-2 sp) twice, ch 1, tr in last dc: 14 tr and 4 sps.

Note: Mark Row 2 as **right** side.

Row 3: Ch 5, turn; tr in next ch-1 sp, ch 2, work Cluster, ch 2, ★ (tr, ch 3, tr) in next ch-3 sp, ch 2, work Cluster, ch 2; repeat from ★ once **more**, tr in next ch-1 sp, ch 1, tr in last tr: 11 sts and 10 sps.

Row 4: Ch 5, turn; 2 tr in next ch-1 sp, tr in next tr, 2 tr in next ch-2 sp, tr in next Cluster, 2 tr in next ch-2 sp, tr in next tr, ★ (2 tr, ch 3, 2 tr) in next ch-3 sp, tr in next tr, 2 tr in next ch-2 sp, tr in next Cluster, 2 tr in next ch-2 sp, tr in next tr; repeat from ★ once **more**, 2 tr in next ch-1 sp, ch 1, tr in last tr; finish off: 35 tr and 4 sps.

28

Continued on page 45.

ABUNDANT CLUSTERS COME TOGETHER TO CREATE A WISPY ARRANGEMENT OF HEXAGON FLORAL MOTIFS ON THIS ELEGANT SUMMER AFGHAN. WORKED IN WORSTED WEIGHT YARN, THE LACY THROW IS AS LOVELY AS IT IS COMFY.

Fresh As A Daisy

Finished Size: 49" x 72"

MATERIALS
Worsted Weight Brushed Acrylic Yarn:
  Green - 38 ounces,
    (1,080 grams, 2,410 yards)
  White - 19 ounces, (540 grams, 1,205 yards)
  Yellow - 4 ounces, (110 grams, 255 yards)
Crochet hook, size G (4.00 mm) **or** size needed
  for gauge

GAUGE SWATCH: 7³/₄" (straight edge to straight edge)
Work same as Motif.

STITCH GUIDE

DOUBLE TREBLE CROCHET
YO 3 times, insert hook in sp indicated, YO
and pull up a loop (5 loops on hook), (YO and
draw through 2 loops on hook) 4 times.

BEGINNING CLUSTER
Ch 3, ★ YO twice, insert hook in sp indicated,
YO and pull up a loop, (YO and draw through
2 loops on hook) twice; repeat from ★ once
more, YO and draw through all 3 loops on
hook.

CLUSTER
★ YO twice, insert hook in sc or sp indicated,
YO and pull up a loop, (YO and draw through
2 loops on hook) twice; repeat from ★ 2 times
more, YO and draw through all 4 loops on
hook.

MOTIF (Make 60)
With Yellow, ch 8; join with slip st to form a ring.

Rnd 1 (Right side): Ch 1, 18 sc in ring; join with
slip st to first sc.

Note: Loop a short piece of yarn around any stitch
to mark Rnd 1 as **right** side.

Rnd 2: Ch 1, sc in same st, ch 5, skip next 2 sc,
(sc in next sc, ch 5, skip next 2 sc) around; join
with slip st to first sc, finish off: 6 ch-5 sps.

Rnd 3: With **right** side facing, join White with
slip st in any ch-5 sp; ch 5 **(counts as first dtr)**,
7 dtr in same sp, 8 dtr in each ch-5 sp around;
join with slip st to first dtr: 48 dtr.

Rnd 4: Ch 1, sc in same st and in next 7 dtr, ch 3,
(sc in next 8 dtr, ch 3) around; join with slip st to
first sc, finish off: 6 ch-3 sps.

Rnd 5: With **right** side facing, join Green with
slip st in any ch-3 sp; work (Beginning Cluster,
ch 5, Cluster) in same sp, ch 3, skip next 2 sc,
(work Cluster in next sc, ch 3, skip next 2 sc)
twice, ★ work (Cluster, ch 5, Cluster) in next
ch-3 sp, ch 3, skip next 2 sc, (work Cluster in next
sc, ch 3, skip next 2 sc) twice; repeat from ★
around; join with slip st to top of Beginning
Cluster: 6 ch-5 sps and 18 ch-3 sps.

Rnd 6: Slip st in first ch-5 sp, ch 1, (3 sc, ch 3,
3 sc) in same sp, 3 sc in each ch-3 sp across to
next ch-5 sp, ★ (3 sc, ch 3, 3 sc) in ch-5 sp, 3 sc
in each ch-3 sp across to next ch-5 sp; repeat from
★ around; join with slip st to first sc: 90 sc.

Rnd 7: Ch 1, sc in same st and in next 2 sc, 3 sc
in next ch-3 sp, ★ sc in each sc across to next
ch-3 sp, 3 sc in ch-3 sp; repeat from ★ 4 times
more, sc in each sc across; join with slip st to first
sc, finish off: 108 sc.

ASSEMBLY
Afghan is assembled by joining Motifs together
forming 4 vertical strips of 9 Motifs each and
3 vertical strips of 8 Motifs each and then by
joining strips.
Join Motifs as follows: With **wrong** sides together
and working through **both** loops of **both** pieces,
join Green with slip st in center sc of first 3-sc
group; ch 1, (slip st in next sc, ch 1) across to
center sc of next 3-sc group, slip st in center sc;
finish off.
Using Placement Diagram, page 45, as a guide,
join strips in same manner.

Continued on page 45.

Garden Drama

Finished Size: 45" x 60"

MATERIALS

Worsted Weight Yarn:
- Ecru - 27 ounces, (770 grams, 1,575 yards)
- Dk Pink - 19 ounces,
  (540 grams, 1,110 yards)
- Pink - 7 ounces, (200 grams, 410 yards)
- Green - 7 ounces, (200 grams, 410 yards)
- Lt Pink - 6 ounces, (170 grams, 350 yards)

Crochet hook, size G (4.00 mm) **or** size needed for gauge

Yarn needle

GAUGE SWATCH: 8¹/₂" (straight edge to straight edge)
Work same as Motif.

STITCH GUIDE

> **TREBLE CROCHET** *(abbreviated tr)*
> YO twice, insert hook in st or sp indicated, YO and pull up a loop (4 loops on hook), (YO and draw through 2 loops on hook) 3 times.
>
> **FRONT POST DOUBLE CROCHET**
> *(abbreviated FPdc)*
> YO, insert hook from **front** to **back** around post of sc indicated *(Fig. 4, page 143)*, YO and pull up a loop (3 loops on hook), (YO and draw through 2 loops on hook) twice.
>
> **PICOT**
> Ch 3, slip st in third ch from hook.
>
> **DECREASE** (uses next 2 sts)
> ★ YO, insert hook in **next** st, YO and pull up a loop, YO and draw through 2 loops on hook; repeat from ★ once **more**, YO and draw through all 3 loops on hook **(counts as one dc).**
>
> **DOUBLE DECREASE** (uses next 3 sts)
> ★ YO, insert hook in **next** st, YO and pull up a loop, YO and draw through 2 loops on hook; repeat from ★ 2 times **more**, YO and draw through all 4 loops on hook **(counts as one dc).**

MOTIF (Make 23)

With Lt Pink, ch 6; join with slip st to form a ring.

Rnd 1 (Right side)**:** Ch 3 **(counts as first dc, now and throughout)**, 17 dc in ring; join with slip st to first dc: 18 dc.

Note: Loop a short piece of yarn around any stitch to mark Rnd 1 as **right** side.

Rnd 2: Ch 1, sc in same st, ch 5, skip next 2 dc, ★ sc in next dc, ch 5, skip next 2 dc; repeat from ★ around; join with slip st to first sc: 6 sc and 6 ch-5 sps.

Rnd 3: Working **behind** ch-5 sps and in skipped dc on Rnd 1 *(Fig. 6, page 143)*, slip st in next dc, ch 3, dc in next dc, ch 8, (dc in next 2 dc, ch 8) around; join with slip st to first dc, finish off: 12 dc and 6 ch-8 sps.

Rnd 4: With **right** side facing, join Pink with sc in any ch-5 sp on Rnd 2 *(see Joining With Sc, page 142)*; (3 dc, ch 2, 3 dc, sc) in same sp **(Petal made)**, ★ ch 1, (sc, 3 dc, ch 2, 3 dc, sc) in next ch-5 sp; repeat from ★ 4 times **more**, sc in first sc to form last ch-1 sp: 6 Petals and 6 ch-1 sps.

Rnd 5: Working around posts of sc on Rnd 2 and keeping ch-6 sps **behind** Petals, work FPdc around sc **below** same st, ch 6, ★ work FPdc around sc **below** next ch-1, ch 6; repeat from ★ around; join with slip st to first FPdc, finish off: 6 FPdc and 6 ch-6 sps.

Rnd 6: With **right** side facing, join Dk Pink with sc in any ch-6 sp; (5 dc, work Picot, 5 dc, sc) in same sp **(Petal made)**, sc in ch-1 sp on Rnd 4 **behind** next FPdc, ★ (sc, 5 dc, work Picot, 5 dc, sc) in next ch-6 sp, sc in ch-1 sp on Rnd 4 **behind** next FPdc; repeat from ★ around; join with slip st to first sc, finish off: 6 Petals.

Rnd 7: With **right** side facing, join Green with sc in any ch-8 sp; in same sp work (2 dc, 2 tr, ch 1, 2 tr, 2 dc, sc) **(Leaf made)**, sc in sp **between** next 2 dc *(Fig. 5, page 143)*, ★ in next ch-8 sp work (sc, 2 dc, 2 tr, ch 1, 2 tr, 2 dc, sc), sc in sp **between** next 2 dc; repeat from ★ around; join with slip st to first sc; do **not** finish off: 66 sts and 6 ch-1 sps.

Continued on page 34.

Rnd 8: Slip st in next dc, ch 1, sc in same st and in next 3 sts, 3 sc in next ch-1 sp, sc in next 4 sts, skip next sc, sc in next sc, skip next sc, ★ sc in next 4 sts, 3 sc in next ch-1 sp, sc in next 4 sts, skip next sc, sc in next sc, skip next st; repeat from ★ around; join with slip st to first sc, finish off: 72 sc.

Rnd 9: With **right** side facing, join Ecru with slip st in center sc of 3-sc group at tip of any Leaf; sc in next sc, hdc in next 2 sc, dc in next 2 sc, tr in next sc, dc in next 2 sc, hdc in next 2 sc, sc in next sc, ★ slip st in next sc, sc in next sc, hdc in next 2 sc, dc in next 2 sc, tr in next sc, dc in next 2 sc, hdc in next 2 sc, sc in next sc; repeat from ★ around; join with slip st to first slip st.

Rnd 10: Ch 3, (2 dc, ch 1, 3 dc) in same st, ch 1, skip next 2 sts, 3 dc in next hdc, ch 1, skip next 2 dc, 3 dc in next tr, ch 1, skip next 2 dc, 3 dc in next hdc, ch 1, skip next 2 sts, ★ (3 dc, ch 1) twice in next slip st, skip next 2 sts, 3 dc in next hdc, ch 1, skip next 2 dc, 3 dc in next tr, ch 1, skip next 2 dc, 3 dc in next hdc, ch 1, skip next 2 sts; repeat from ★ around; join with slip st to first dc: 30 ch-1 sps.

Rnd 11: Slip st in next 2 dc and in next ch-1 sp, ch 3, (2 dc, ch 1, 3 dc) in same sp, ch 1, (3 dc in next ch-1 sp, ch 1) across to next corner ch-1 sp, ★ (3 dc, ch 1) twice in corner ch-1 sp, (3 dc in next ch-1 sp, ch 1) across to next corner ch-1 sp; repeat from ★ around; join with slip st to first dc: 36 ch-1 sps.

Rnd 12: Slip st in next 2 dc and in next ch-1 sp, ch 3, (2 dc, ch 1, 3 dc) in same sp, 3 dc in each ch-1 sp across to next corner ch-1 sp, ★ (3 dc, ch 1, 3 dc) in corner ch-1 sp, 3 dc in each ch-1 sp across to next corner ch-1 sp; repeat from ★ around; join with slip st to first dc, finish off: 126 dc and 6 ch-1 sps.

Rnd 13: With **right** side facing, join Dk Pink with sc in any corner ch-1 sp; 2 sc in same sp, sc in each dc across to next ch-1 sp, ★ 3 sc in ch-1 sp, sc in each dc across to next ch-1 sp; repeat from ★ around; join with slip st to first sc, finish off: 144 sc.

HALF MOTIF (Make 4)

With Ecru, ch 6 **loosely**.

Row 1: Sc in second ch from hook and in each ch across: 5 sc.

Row 2 (Right side)**:** Ch 3, turn; 2 dc in same st, (ch 1, skip next sc, 3 dc in next sc) twice: 9 dc and 2 ch-1 sps.

Note: Mark Row 2 as **right** side.

Row 3: Ch 3, turn; 2 dc in same st, (3 dc, ch 1, 3 dc) in each of next 2 ch-1 sps, 3 dc in last dc: 18 dc and 2 ch-1 sps.

Row 4: Ch 3, turn; 2 dc in same st, skip next 2 dc, 3 dc in sp **before** next dc, ★ (3 dc, ch 1, 3 dc) in next ch-1 sp, skip next 3 dc, 3 dc in sp **before** next dc; repeat from ★ once **more**, skip next 2 dc, 3 dc in last dc: 27 dc and 2 ch-1 sps.

Rows 5-8: Ch 3, turn; 2 dc in same st, skip next 2 dc, † (3 dc in sp **before** next dc, skip next 3 dc) across to next ch-1 sp, (3 dc, ch 1, 3 dc) in ch-1 sp †, skip next 3 dc, repeat from † to † once, (skip next 3 dc, 3 dc in sp **before** next dc) across to last 3 dc, skip next 2 dc, 3 dc in last dc: 63 dc and 2 ch-1 sps.

Finish off.

Edging: With **right** side facing, join Dk Pink with sc in first dc; 2 sc in same st and in next dc, ★ sc in each dc across to next ch-1 sp, 3 sc in ch-1 sp; repeat from ★ once **more**, sc in each dc across to last 2 dc, 2 sc in next dc, 3 sc in last dc; work 44 sc evenly spaced across end of rows; join with slip st to first sc, finish off: 119 sc.

ASSEMBLY

When joining Motifs or Strips, use Dk Pink and work through **both** loops to whipstitch pieces together *(Fig. 9a, page 144)*.

To whipstitch Motifs, begin in center sc of first corner and end in center sc of next corner.

To whipstitch Strip to Ripple, begin in center sc of first corner on Strip and first sc on Ripple and end in center sc of last corner on Strip and last sc on Ripple *(see Placement Diagram, page 36)*.

STRIP A

Whipstitch 5 Motifs together. Add Ripple A.

RIPPLE A

Row 1: With **right** side facing and working across long edge of Strip A, join Dk Pink with sc in center sc of top right corner; sc in each sc and in each joining across to center sc of next corner, sc in center sc: 241 sc.

Row 2: Ch 3, turn; decrease, dc in next 21 sc, 3 dc in next sc, ★ dc in next 22 sc, double decrease, dc in next 22 sc, 3 dc in next sc; repeat from ★ 3 times **more**, dc in next 21 sc, decrease, dc in last sc; finish off.

Row 3: With **right** side facing, join Pink with sc in first dc; skip next dc, sc in next 22 dc, 3 sc in next dc, ★ sc in next 23 dc, skip next 2 dc, sc in next 22 dc, 3 sc in next dc; repeat from ★ 3 times **more**, sc in next 22 dc, skip next dc, sc in last dc.

Row 4: Ch 3, turn; decrease, dc in next 21 sc, 3 dc in next sc, ★ dc in next 22 sc, double decrease, dc in next 22 sc, 3 dc in next sc; repeat from ★ 3 times **more**, dc in next 21 sc, decrease, dc in last sc; finish off.

Rows 5 and 6: With Lt Pink, repeat Rows 3 and 4.

Rows 7 and 8: With Ecru, repeat Rows 3 and 4.

Do **not** finish off.

Row 9: Ch 1, turn; sc in first dc, skip next dc, sc in next 22 dc, 3 sc in next dc, ★ sc in next 23 dc, skip next 2 dc, sc in next 22 dc, 3 sc in next dc; repeat from ★ 3 times **more**, sc in next 22 dc, skip next dc, sc in last dc.

Row 10: Repeat Row 4.

Row 11: With **right** side facing, join Dk Pink with sc in first dc; sc in each dc across; finish off.

STRIP B

Whipstitch 4 Motifs together adding a Half Motif on each end. Whipstitch Strip B to Ripple A. Add Ripple B.

RIPPLE B

Row 1: With **right** side facing and working across long edge of Strip B, join Dk Pink with sc in center sc of top right corner; sc in each sc and in each joining across to center sc of next corner, sc in center sc: 241 sc.

Row 2: Ch 3, turn; dc in same st and in next 22 sc, double decrease, dc in next 22 sc, ★ 3 dc in next sc, dc in next 22 sc, double decrease, dc in next 22 sc; repeat from ★ across to last sc, 2 dc in last sc; finish off.

Row 3: With **right** side facing, join Pink with sc in first dc; sc in same st and in next 23 dc, skip next 2 dc, sc in next 22 dc, ★ 3 sc in next dc, sc in next 23 dc, skip next 2 dc, sc in next 22 dc; repeat from ★ across to last dc, 2 sc in last dc.

Row 4: Ch 3, turn; dc in same st and in next 22 sc, double decrease, dc in next 22 sc, ★ 3 dc in next sc, dc in next 22 sc, double decrease, dc in next 22 sc; repeat from ★ across to last sc, 2 dc in last sc; finish off.

Rows 5 and 6: With Lt Pink, repeat Rows 3 and 4.

Rows 7 and 8: With Ecru, repeat Rows 3 and 4.

Do **not** finish off.

Row 9: Ch 1, turn; 2 sc in first sc, sc in next 23 dc, skip next 2 dc, sc in next 22 dc, ★ 3 sc in next dc, sc in next 23 dc, skip next 2 dc, sc in next 22 dc; repeat from ★ across to last dc, 2 sc in last dc.

Row 10: Repeat Row 4.

Row 11: With **right** side facing, join Dk Pink with sc in first dc; sc in each dc across; finish off.

STRIP C

Whipstitch 5 Motifs together. Whipstitch Strip C to Ripple B. Add Ripple C.

RIPPLE C

Row 1: With **right** side facing and working across long edge of Strip C, join Dk Pink with sc in center sc of top right corner; sc in each sc and in each joining across to center sc of next corner, sc in center sc: 241 sc.

Rows 2-11: Work same as Ripple A.

STRIP D

Whipstitch 4 Motifs together adding a Half Motif on each end. Whipstitch Strip D to Ripple C. Add Ripple D.

Continued on page 36.

RIPPLE D

Row 1: With **right** side facing and working across long edge of Strip D, join Dk Pink with sc in center sc of top right corner; sc in each sc and in each joining across to center sc of next corner, sc in center sc: 241 sc.

Rows 2-11: Work same as Ripple B.

STRIP E

Whipstitch 5 Motifs together. Whipstitch Strip E to Ripple D.

PLACEMENT DIAGRAM

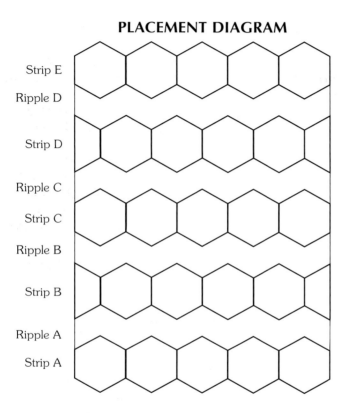

Strip E
Ripple D

Strip D

Ripple C

Strip C

Ripple B

Strip B

Ripple A

Strip A

EDGING

Rnd 1: With **right** side facing, join Dk Pink with sc in any sc; sc evenly around working 3 sc in center sc of each corner; join with slip st to first sc.

Rnd 2: Ch 3, turn; dc evenly around working 3 dc in center sc of each corner; join with slip st to first dc.

Rnd 3: Ch 1, turn; sc evenly around working 3 sc in center dc of each corner; join with slip st to first sc, finish off.

Design by Lissa Ammann.

BLUEBERRY TWIST

Continued from page 10.

from ★ 16 times **more**, 4 dc in each of next 2 sps, (3 dc, 3 tr) in next ch-4 sp †, (3 tr, 3 dc) in next ch-4 sp, repeat from † to † once working tr around Foundation ch **between** legs of tr on opposite side; join with slip st to first tr, finish off: 500 sts.

Rnd 3: With **right** side facing, skip first 3 tr and join Ecru with sc *(see Joining With Sc, page 142)* in sp **before** next dc *(Fig. 5, page 143)*; sc in sp **before** each of next 2 dc, † (work FPdc around next Popcorn on Rnd 1, skip next 2 sts behind FPdc, sc in sp **before** each of next 3 dc) twice, ★ work FPdc Cluster, skip next 3 sts behind FPdc Cluster, sc in sp **before** each of next 3 dc, (work FPdc around next Popcorn on Rnd 1, skip next 2 sts behind FPdc, sc in sp **before** each of next 3 sts) twice; repeat from ★ 17 times **more**, work FPtr around Beginning Popcorn on Foundation Row, skip tr behind FPtr, (sc in next tr, sc in sp **before** next tr, sc in next tr, work FPtr around same Beginning Popcorn as last FPtr) twice, skip tr behind FPtr †, sc in sp **before** each of next 3 dc, repeat from † to † once; join with slip st to first sc, finish off: 472 sts.

Rnd 4: With **right** side facing and working in Back Loops Only *(Fig. 2, page 143)*, join Lt Green with sc in same st as joining; sc in next 7 sts, † hdc in next sc, dc in next 2 sc, tr in next FPdc Cluster, dc in next 2 sc, hdc in next sc, ★ sc in next 5 sts, hdc in next sc, dc in next 2 sc, tr in next FPdc Cluster, dc in next 2 sc, hdc in next sc; repeat from ★ 16 times **more**, sc in next 8 sts, 2 sc in next FPtr, sc in next 7 sts, 2 sc in next FPtr †, sc in next 8 sts, repeat from † to † once; join with slip st to **both** loops of first sc, do **not** finish off: 476 sts.

Rnd 5: Ch 1, working in both loops, sc in same st and in next 3 sc, † place marker in last sc made for joining placement, sc in next 220 sts, place marker in last sc made for joining placement, sc in next 3 sc, 2 sc in next sc, sc in next 9 sc, 2 sc in next sc †, sc in next 4 sc, repeat from † to † once; join with slip st to first sc, finish off.

ASSEMBLY

With **wrong** sides together, using Lt Green and working through **both** loops, whipstitch Strips together *(Fig. 9a, page 144)*, beginning in first marked sc and ending in next marked sc.

Design by Tammy Kreimeyer.

PRIMROSE PATCH

Continued from page 12.

Rnd 8 (Joining rnd)**:** Using Placement Diagram as a guide, work One, Two, or Three Side Joining, arranging Motifs into 4 horizontal strips of 11 Motifs each and 5 horizontal strips of 10 Motifs each.

ONE SIDE JOINING

Rnd 8 (Joining rnd)**:** Work Beginning Cluster, ch 3, dc in next ch-3 sp and in next dc, ★ (dc, ch 3, dc) in next ch-1 sp, dc in next dc and in next ch-3 sp, ch 3, work Cluster, ch 3, dc in next ch-3 sp and in next dc; repeat from ★ 3 times **more**, dc in next ch-1 sp, ch 2, holding Motifs with **right** sides facing, drop loop from hook, insert hook from **front** to **back** in corresponding ch-3 sp on **adjacent Motif**, hook dropped loop and draw through, ch 1, dc in same sp on **new Motif**, dc in next dc and in next ch-3 sp, ch 3, work Cluster, drop loop from hook, insert hook from **front** to **back** in next Cluster on **adjacent Motif**, hook dropped loop and draw through, ch 3, dc in next ch-3 sp on **new Motif**, dc in next dc and in next ch-1 sp, ch 2, drop loop from hook, insert hook from **front** to **back** in next ch-3 sp on **adjacent Motif**, hook dropped loop and draw through, ch 1, dc in same sp on **new Motif**, dc in next dc and in next ch-3 sp, ch 3; join with slip st to top of Beginning Cluster, finish off.

TWO SIDE JOINING

Rnd 8 (Joining rnd)**:** Work Beginning Cluster, ch 3, dc in next ch-3 sp and in next dc, ★ (dc, ch 3, dc) in next ch-1 sp, dc in next dc and in next ch-3 sp, ch 3, work Cluster, ch 3, dc in next ch-3 sp and in next dc; repeat from ★ 2 times **more**, dc in next ch-1 sp, ch 2, holding Motifs with **right** sides facing, drop loop from hook, insert hook from **front** to **back** in corresponding ch-3 sp on **adjacent Motif**, hook dropped loop and draw through, ch 1, dc in same sp on **new Motif**, dc in next dc and in next ch-3 sp, † ch 3, work Cluster, drop loop from hook, insert hook from **front** to **back** in next Cluster on **adjacent Motif**, hook dropped loop and draw through, ch 3, dc in next ch-3 sp on **new Motif**, dc in next dc and in next ch-1 sp, ch 2, drop loop from hook, insert hook from **front** to **back** in next ch-3 sp on **adjacent**

Motif, hook dropped loop and draw through, ch 1, dc in same sp on **new Motif**, dc in next dc and in next ch-3 sp, ch 3 †; repeat from † to † once **more**; join with slip st to top of Beginning Cluster, finish off.

THREE SIDE JOINING

Rnd 8 (Joining rnd)**:** Work Beginning Cluster, ch 3, dc in next ch-3 sp and in next dc, ★ (dc, ch 3, dc) in next ch-1 sp, dc in next dc and in next ch-3 sp, ch 3, work Cluster, ch 3, dc in next ch-3 sp and in next dc; repeat from ★ once **more**, dc in next ch-1 sp, ch 2, holding Motifs with **right** sides facing, drop loop from hook, insert hook from **front** to **back** in corresponding ch-3 sp on **adjacent Motif**, hook dropped loop and draw through, ch 1, dc in same sp on **new Motif**, dc in next dc and in next ch-3 sp, ch 3, † work Cluster, drop loop from hook, insert hook from **front** to **back** in next Cluster on **adjacent Motif**, hook dropped loop and draw through, ch 3, dc in next ch-3 sp on **new Motif**, dc in next dc and in next ch-1 sp, ch 2, drop loop from hook, insert hook from **front** to **back** in next ch-3 sp on **adjacent Motif**, hook dropped loop and draw through, ch 1, dc in same sp on **new Motif**, dc in next dc and in next ch-3 sp, ch 3 †; repeat from † to † 2 times **more**; join with slip st to top of Beginning Cluster, finish off.

PLACEMENT DIAGRAM

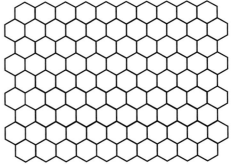

EDGING

With **right** side facing, join Green with slip st in any dc; ch 1, sc evenly around entire Afghan; join with slip st to first sc, finish off.

Design by Terry Kimbrough.

SUMMER SUNFLOWERS

Continued from page 14.

Rnd 3: Slip st in first ch-2 sp, work (Beginning Popcorn, ch 1, Popcorn) in same sp, ch 1, (work Popcorn, ch 1) twice in each ch-2 sp around; join with slip st to top of Beginning Popcorn, finish off: 24 Popcorns and 24 ch-1 sps.

Rnd 4: With **right** side facing and working in Front Loops Only **(Fig. 2, page 143)**, join Gold with slip st in any ch; (work Petal, slip st) in same st, sc in next ch, ★ (slip st, work Petal, slip st) in next ch, sc in next ch; repeat from ★ around; join with slip st to first slip st: 12 Petals.

Rnd 5: Working **behind** Petals and in free loops of sts on Rnd 3 **(Fig. 3a, page 143)**, (slip st in next ch, ch 5, skip next ch) around; join with slip st to first slip st: 12 ch-5 sps.

Rnd 6: Slip st in next 2 chs, work Petal in same ch-5 sp, slip st in fourth ch of same ch-5, ch 3, ★ skip first ch of next ch-5, slip st in next ch, work Petal in same ch-5 sp, slip st in fourth ch of same ch-5, ch 3; repeat from ★ around, skip last ch and first slip st; join with slip st to next slip st, finish off: 12 Petals and 12 ch-3 sps.

Rnd 7: With **right** side facing, join Green with sc in any Picot **(see Joining With Sc, page 142)**; ch 1, tr in next ch-3 sp, sc in next Picot on Rnd 4, tr in same sp as last tr made, ch 1, ★ sc in next Picot on Rnd 6, ch 1, tr in next ch-3 sp, sc in next Picot on Rnd 4, tr in same sp as last tr made, ch 1; repeat from ★ around; join with slip st to first sc, finish off: 48 sts and 24 ch-1 sps.

Rnd 8: With **right** side facing, join Blue with sc in same st as joining; ch 2, dc in next tr, work FPdc around next sc, dc in next tr, ch 2, ★ sc in next sc, ch 2, dc in next tr, work FPdc around next sc, dc in next tr, ch 2; repeat from ★ around; join with slip st to first sc, finish off.

Rnd 9: With **right** side facing, join Green with slip st in same st as joining; ch 6 **(counts as first dc plus ch 3)**, dc in same st, ch 1, dc in next dc, work FPdc around next FPdc, dc in next dc, ch 1, (dc, ch 1) twice in next sc, dc in next dc, work FPdc around next FPdc, dc in next dc, ch 1, ★ (dc, ch 3, dc) in next sc, ch 1, dc in next dc, work FPdc around next FPdc, dc in next dc, ch 1, (dc, ch 1) twice in next sc, dc in next dc, work FPdc around next FPdc, dc in next dc, ch 1; repeat from ★ around; join with slip st to first dc, finish off: 60 sts and 36 sps.

HALF MOTIF (Make 8)

With Brown, ch 4; join with slip st to form a ring.

Row 1 (Right side)**:** Ch 3 **(counts as first dc)**, work Popcorn in ring, (ch 2, work Popcorn in ring) twice, dc in ring: 3 Popcorns and 2 ch-2 sps.

Note: Mark Row 1 as **right** side.

Row 2: Turn; work Beginning Popcorn in first dc, ch 2, (work Popcorn, ch 2) twice in next 2 ch-2 sps, work Popcorn in last dc: 6 Popcorns and 5 ch-2 sps.

Push Popcorns to **right** side.

Row 3: Turn, work Beginning Popcorn in first Popcorn, ch 1, (work Popcorn, ch 1) twice in next 5 ch-2 sps, work Popcorn in last Popcorn, finish off: 12 Popcorns and 11 ch-1 sps.

Row 4: With **right** side facing and working in Front Loops Only, join Gold with sc in first Popcorn; (slip st, work Petal, slip st) in next ch, ★ sc in next ch, (slip st, work Petal, slip st) in next ch; repeat from ★ 4 times **more**, sc in last Popcorn: 6 Petals.

Row 5: Ch 3, turn; working in **front** of Petals and in free loops of sts on Row 3, slip st in first ch, ★ ch 5, skip next ch, slip st in next ch; repeat from ★ 4 times **more**, ch 3, slip st in last sc: 7 sps.

Row 6: Ch 1, turn; slip st in first 2 chs, [ch 3, tr in same ch-3 sp, work Picot, ch 3, slip st in same ch on Row 5 as last slip st made **(Petal made)**], ch 3, ★ skip first ch of next ch-5, slip st in next ch, work Petal in same ch-5 sp, slip st in fourth ch of same ch-5, ch 3; repeat from ★ across to last ch-3 sp, slip st in center ch of last ch-3, ch 3, tr in same ch-3 sp, work Picot, ch 3, slip st in same ch on Row 5 as last slip st made; finish off.

Row 7: With **right** side facing, join Green with sc in first Picot; ★ ch 1, tr in next ch-3 sp, sc in next Picot on Row 4, tr in same sp as last tr made, ch 1, sc in next Picot on Row 6; repeat from ★ across; finish off: 25 sts and 12 ch-1 sps.

Row 8: With **right** side facing, join Blue with sc in first sc; ★ ch 2, dc in next tr, work FPdc around next sc, dc in next tr, ch 2, sc in next sc; repeat from ★ across; finish off.

38

Row 9: With **right** side facing, join Green with slip st in first sc; ch 4 **(counts as first dc plus ch 1)**, dc in same st, ch 1, dc in next dc, work FPdc around next FPdc, dc in next dc, ch 1, (dc, ch 1) twice in next sc, dc in next dc, work FPdc around next FPdc, dc in next dc, ★ ch 1, (dc, ch 3, dc) in next sc, ch 1, dc in next dc, work FPdc around next FPdc, dc in next dc, ch 1, (dc, ch 1) twice in next sc, dc in next dc, work FPdc around next FPdc, dc in next dc; repeat from ★ once **more**, (ch 1, dc) twice in last sc; finish off: 32 sts and 19 sps.

ASSEMBLY

Keep working yarn to **wrong** side of Afghan.

With Gold, using Placement Diagram as a guide, and working Slip St Joining **(Fig. 1, page 14)**, join Motifs together forming 5 horizontal strips of 6 Motifs each and 4 horizontal strips of 5 Motifs and 2 Half Motifs, beginning in center ch of first corner ch-3 and ending in center ch of next corner ch-3; then join strips together, beginning in first dc on Half Motif and center ch of corner ch-3 on Motif and ending in last dc on Half Motif and center ch of next corner ch-3 on last Motif.

PLACEMENT DIAGRAM

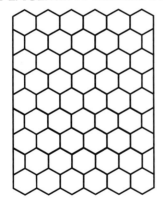

EDGING

Rnd 1: With **right** side facing and working in Front Loops Only, join Gold with sc in center ch of any corner ch-3; ch 1, sc in same st, sc evenly around entire Afghan working (sc, ch 1, sc) in center ch of each unworked ch-3 around; join with slip st to first sc.

Rnd 2: Ch 1, sc in same st and in each sc around working (sc, ch 1, sc) in each ch-1 sp; join with slip st to first sc, finish off.

Design by Tammy Kreimeyer.

GRANNY'S ZINNIAS

Continued from page 16.

ASSEMBLY

Using Placement Diagram as a guide and Rose, whipstitch Squares together **(Fig. 9a, page 144)**, beginning in center ch of first corner ch-3 and ending in center ch of next corner ch-3, forming 5 vertical strips of 19 Small Squares each and 4 vertical strips of 6 Large Squares and 14 Small Squares each; then whipstitch strips together in same manner.

PLACEMENT DIAGRAM

B	A	A	B	A	A	B	A	A	B	A	A	B
A			A			A			A			A
A			A			A			A			A
B	A	A	B	A	A	B	A	A	B	A	A	B
A			A			A			A			A
A			A			A			A			A
B	A	A	B	A	A	B	A	A	B	A	A	B
A			A			A			A			A
A			A			A			A			A
B	A	A	B	A	A	B	A	A	B	A	A	B
A			A			A			A			A
A			A			A			A			A
B	A	A	B	A	A	B	A	A	B	A	A	B
A			A			A			A			A
A			A			A			A			A
B	A	A	B	A	A	B	A	A	B	A	A	B
A			A			A			A			A
A			A			A			A			A
B	A	A	B	A	A	B	A	A	B	A	A	B

EDGING

Rnd 1: With **right** side facing, join Rose with sc in any corner ch-3 sp **(see Joining With Sc, page 142)**; ch 2, sc in same sp, ★ † ch 1, skip next dc, sc in next dc, ch 1, (sc in next ch-1 sp, ch 1, skip next dc, sc in next dc, ch 1) twice, [(sc in next sp, ch 1) twice, skip next dc, sc in next dc, ch 1, (sc in next ch-1 sp, ch 1, skip next dc, sc in next dc, ch 1) twice] across to next corner ch-3 sp †, (sc, ch 2, sc) in ch-3 sp; repeat from ★ 2 times **more**, then repeat from † to † once; join with slip st to first sc.

Rnd 2: Slip st in first ch-2 sp, ch 1, (sc, ch 2, sc) in same sp, ch 1, (sc in next ch-1 sp, ch 1) across to next ch-2 sp, ★ (sc, ch 2, sc) in ch-2 sp, ch 1, (sc in next ch-1 sp, ch 1) across to next ch-2 sp; repeat from ★ around; join with slip st to first sc.

Rnd 3: (Slip st, ch 1) twice in first ch-2 sp, (slip st in next ch-1 sp, ch 1) across to next ch-2 sp, ★ (slip st, ch 1) twice in ch-2 sp, (slip st in next ch-1 sp, ch 1) across to next ch-2 sp; repeat from ★ around; join with slip st to first slip st, finish off.

Design by Anne Halliday.

RICH BLOSSOMS

Continued from page 18.

ASSEMBLY

With Ecru, using Placement Diagram as a guide, and working through **inside** loops, whipstitch Triangles together forming 10 horizontal strips of 13 Triangles each *(Fig. 9b, page 144)*, beginning in first corner sc, ending in next corner sc, and leaving ch-3 sps unworked; then whipstitch strips together in same manner.

PLACEMENT DIAGRAM
KEY

△ Pink   ▲ Dk Blue

▲ Dk Pink   ▲ Purple

△ Blue   ▲ Dk Purple

● Point A

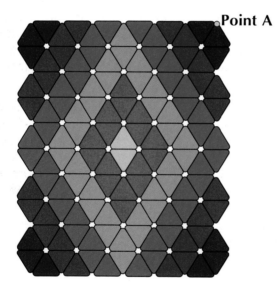

FILL-IN MOTIF

With Ecru, ch 4; join with slip st to form a ring.

Rnd 1: Ch 1, sc in ring, ch 1; with **right** side of Afghan facing and working in any intersection of 6 Triangles, sc in any ch-3 sp, ch 1, ★ sc in ring, ch 1, sc in next ch-3 sp, ch 1; repeat from ★ 4 times **more**; join with slip st to first sc, finish off.

Repeat for each space between joined Triangles.

EDGING

With **right** side of short end facing and working in Back Loops Only *(Fig. 2, page 143)*, join Ecru with slip st in top right corner ch-3 sp (Point A on Placement Diagram); ch 3, dc in same sp, ch 1,

2 dc in next ch-3 sp, ch 1, † sc in next sc, ch 1, (skip next st, sc in next st, ch 1) across to next ch-3 sp, [dc in next ch-3 sp, tr in next ch-3 sp, dc in next ch-3 sp, ch 1, sc in next sc, ch 1, (skip next st, sc in next st, ch 1) across to next ch-3 sp] 5 times, [(2 dc in next ch-3 sp, ch 1) twice, sc in next sc, ch 1, (skip next st, sc in next st, ch 1) across to next ch-3 sp] twice, ★ dc in next ch-3 sp, decrease, dc in next ch-3 sp, ch 1, sc in next sc, ch 1, (skip next st, sc in next st, ch 1) across to next ch-3 sp, (2 dc in next ch-3 sp, ch 1) twice, sc in next sc, ch 1, (skip next st, sc in next st, ch 1) across to next ch-3 sp; repeat from ★ 3 times **more** †, (2 dc in next ch-3 sp, ch 1) twice, repeat from † to † once; join with slip st to first dc, finish off.

Design by Carole Prior.

DAISY DAYS Continued from page 20.

Rnd 2 (Joining rnd)**:** With **right** side facing, join White with slip st in any dc; work Long Petal, work FPsc around same dc as slip st, slip st in next dc, work Short Petal, work FPsc around same dc as slip st, ★ (slip st in next dc, work Long Petal, work FPsc around same dc as slip st) twice, slip st in next dc, work Short Petal, work FPsc around same dc as slip st; repeat from ★ once **more**, place marker around 3 skipped chs at tip of sixth Petal made for joining placement, slip st in next dc, work Long Petal, work FPsc around same dc as slip st, slip st in next dc, ch 7 **loosely**, holding Flowers with **wrong** sides together, slip st in marked ch-3 sp on **previous Flower**, † ch 1, skip next ch on **new Flower**, working in back ridge of chs, sc in next ch, hdc in next ch, dc in next 2 chs, hdc in next ch, sc in last ch, work FPsc around same dc as slip st †, slip st in next dc, ch 6 **loosely**, slip st in ch-3 sp at tip of next Petal on **previous Flower**, ch 1, skip next ch on **new Flower**, working in back ridge of chs, sc in next ch, dc in next 2 chs, hdc in next ch, sc in last ch, work FPsc around same dc as slip st, slip st in next dc, ch 7 **loosely**, slip st in ch-3 sp at tip of next Petal on **previous Flower**, repeat from † to † once; join with slip st to slip st at base of first Petal, finish off: 12 Petals.

LAST FLOWER

With larger size hook and Yellow, ch 4; join with slip st to form a ring.

Rnd 1 (Right side)**:** Ch 3, 11 dc in ring; join with slip st to first dc, finish off: 12 dc.

Note: Mark Rnd 1 as **right** side.

Rnd 2 (Joining rnd)**:** With **right** side facing, join White with slip st in any dc; work Long Petal, work FPsc around same dc as slip st, slip st in next dc, work Short Petal, work FPsc around same dc as slip st, (slip st in next dc, work Long Petal, work FPsc around same dc as slip st) 5 times, place marker around 3 skipped chs at tip of sixth Petal made for joining placement, slip st in next dc, work Short Petal, work FPsc around same dc as slip st, slip st in next dc, work Long Petal, work FPsc around same dc as slip st, slip st in next dc, ch 7 **loosely**, holding Flowers with **wrong** sides together, slip st in marked ch-3 sp on **previous Flower**, † ch 1, skip next ch on **new Flower**, working in back ridge of chs, sc in next ch, hdc in next ch, dc in next 2 chs, hdc in next ch, sc in last ch, work FPsc around same dc as slip st †, slip st in next dc, ch 6 **loosely**, slip st in ch-3 sp at tip of next Petal on **previous Flower**, ch 1, skip next ch on **new Flower**, working in back ridge of chs, sc in next ch, dc in next 2 chs, hdc in next ch, sc in last ch, work FPsc around same dc as slip st, slip st in next dc, ch 7 **loosely**, slip st in ch-3 sp at tip of next Petal on **previous Flower**, repeat from † to † once; join with slip st to slip st at base of first Petal, finish off: 12 Petals.

BORDER

Rnd 1: With **right** side facing and larger size hook, join Lt Green with sc in marked ch-3 sp on last Flower made **(see Joining With Sc, page 142)**; (ch 2, work dc Cluster, ch 2, sc in same sp) 3 times, † ch 3, work Cluster, ch 3, sc in same sp, ★ (ch 2, work dc Cluster, ch 2, sc in same sp) twice, ch 3, work Cluster, ch 3, sc in same sp; repeat from ★ 11 times **more** †, (ch 2, work dc Cluster, ch 2, sc in same sp) 8 times, repeat from † to † once, (ch 2, work dc Cluster, ch 2, sc in same sp) 4 times, ch 2, work dc Cluster working second leg in same sp as first sc, ch 2; join with slip st to first sc: 90 Clusters and 90 sc.

Rnd 2: Ch 1, sc in same st, work Shell in next Cluster, (sc in next sc, work Shell in next Cluster) around; join with slip st to first sc, finish off.

TRIM

Row 1: With **right** side facing and larger size hook, skip first ch-1 sp and join White with sc in next ch-1 sp; sc in same sp and in next dc, decrease, sc in next dc, ★ (sc, ch 1, sc) in next ch-1 sp, sc in next dc, decrease, sc in next dc; repeat from ★ 38 times **more**, 2 sc in next ch-1 sp, leave remaining sts and sps unworked; finish off: 202 sts and 39 ch-1 sps.

Row 2: With **right** side facing, join Yellow with sc in first sc; sc in next sc, hdc in next sc, dc in next decrease, hdc in next sc, ★ sc in next sc, sc in next ch-1 sp and in next sc, hdc in next sc, dc in next decrease, hdc in next sc; repeat from ★ across to last 2 sc, sc in last 2 sc; finish off.

NEXT 5 STRIPS

Work same as First Strip through Trim.

TRIM - SECOND SIDE
Row 1: With **right** side facing and larger size hook, skip 4 ch-1 sps from Trim and join White with sc in next ch-1 sp; sc in same sp and in next dc, decrease, sc in next dc, ★ (sc, ch 1, sc) in next ch-1 sp, sc in next dc, decrease, sc in next dc; repeat from ★ 38 times **more**, 2 sc in next ch-1 sp, leave remaining sts and sps unworked; finish off: 202 sts and 39 ch-1 sps.

Row 2: With **right** side facing, join Yellow with sc in first sc; sc in next sc, hdc in next sc, dc in next decrease, hdc in next sc, ★ sc in next sc, sc in next ch-1 sp and in next sc, hdc in next sc, dc in next decrease, hdc in next sc; repeat from ★ across to last 2 sc, sc in last 2 sc; finish off.

LAST STRIP

Work same as First Strip.

ASSEMBLY

With **wrong** sides together, using Yellow and working through **both** loops on Trim, whipstitch Strips together **(Fig. 9a, page 144)**, beginning in first sc and ending in last sc.

EDGING

With **right** side facing and smaller size hook, join Lt Green with slip st in any ch-1 sp; ch 1, working in sts, sps, and in end of rows, (slip st in next st or sp, ch 1) around; join with slip st to first slip st, finish off.

Design by Tammy Kreimeyer.

PINK CARNATIONS

Continued from page 22.

Rnd 8: With **right** side facing, join Green with slip st in any ch-2 sp; work (Beginning Cluster, ch 2, Cluster) in same sp, sc in each dc across to next ch-2 sp, ★ work (Cluster, ch 2, Cluster) in ch-2 sp, sc in each dc across to next ch-2 sp; repeat from ★ 2 times **more**; join with slip st to top of Beginning Cluster, finish off: 68 sc.

Rnd 9: With **right** side facing, join Lt Green with sc in any ch-2 sp *(see Joining With Sc, page 142)*; 4 sc in same sp, sc in each sc across to next ch-2 sp, ★ 5 sc in ch-2 sp, sc in each sc across to next ch-2 sp; repeat from ★ 2 times **more**; join with slip st to first sc, finish off: 88 sc.

Rnd 10: With **right** side facing, join Ecru with slip st in same st as joining; ch 3, dc in next sc, (2 dc, ch 2, 2 dc) in next sc, ★ dc in each sc across to center sc of next 5-sc group, (2 dc, ch 2, 2 dc) in center sc; repeat from ★ 2 times **more**, dc in each sc across; join with slip st to first dc, finish off: 100 dc and 4 ch-2 sps.

JOINING

Join Squares together forming 3 vertical Panels of 7 Squares each as follows:

With **wrong** sides together, matching sts, and working through inside loop of **each** stitch on **both** pieces, join Lt Green with slip st in second ch of first corner ch-2; ch 1, (slip st in next dc, ch 1) across to next corner ch-2, slip st in next ch; finish off.

STRIP (Make 4)
CENTER

With Pink, ch 6; join with slip st to form a ring.

Row 1 (Right side): Ch 3, (work Popcorn, dc) in ring.

Note: Mark Row 1 as **right** side and bottom edge.

Row 2: Ch 3, turn; skip Popcorn, slip st in sp **before** next dc *(Fig. 5, page 143)*.

Row 3: Ch 3, turn; (work Popcorn, dc) in next ch-3 sp.

Rows 4-130: Repeat Rows 2 and 3, 63 times; then repeat Row 2 once **more**.

Finish off.

LEFT SIDE

Row 1: With **right** side facing, bottom edge to the left, and working in end of rows, join Ecru with slip st in first row; ch 3, 2 dc in next row, (skip next row, 3 dc in next row) across to last 2 rows, skip next row, 2 dc in last row, dc in beginning ring; finish off: 195 dc.

Row 2: With **right** side facing, join Lt Green with sc in first dc; sc in each dc across; finish off.

Row 3: With **right** side facing, join Green with sc in first sc; sc in each sc across; finish off.

Row 4: With **right** side facing, join Ecru with slip st in first sc; ch 3, dc in next sc and in each sc across; finish off.

RIGHT SIDE

Row 1: With **right** side of Center facing and working in end of rows on opposite side of Center, join Ecru with slip st in beginning ring; ch 3, 2 dc in next row, (skip next row, 3 dc in next row) across to last 3 rows, skip next row, 2 dc in next row, dc in last row; finish off: 195 dc.

Rows 2-4: Work same as Left Side.

ASSEMBLY

Afghan is assembled by alternating Strips and Panels in the following sequence: Strip, (Panel, Strip) 3 times.

Join Strips to Panels as follows:

With **wrong** sides and bottom edges of Panel and Strip together, Panel facing you, and working through inside loops of **each** stitch on **both** pieces, join Green with slip st in second ch of first ch-2 on Square and first dc on Strip; ch 1, (slip st in next dc, ch 1) 25 times, ★ slip st in next ch, ch 1, slip st in next joining, ch 1, slip st in next ch, ch 1, (slip st in next dc, ch 1) 25 times; repeat from ★ across to last ch-2 on Panel, slip st in next ch; finish off.

EDGING

With **right** side facing and working across long edge of Afghan, join Lt Green with sc in first dc; sc in same st, † work Picot, (skip next dc, sc in next dc, work Picot) across to last 2 dc, skip next dc, 2 sc in last dc; working in end of rows on first Strip, ch 3, sc in first row, ch 3, skip next 2 rows, sc in next row, ch 3, sc in sp on Center of Strip, ch 3, sc in next row, ch 3, skip next 2 rows, sc in last row, ★ ch 3; working across Panel, sc in first sp, ch 3, (skip next 2 dc, sc in next dc, ch 3) across to last dc, skip last dc, sc in last sp, ch 3; working in end of rows on next Strip, sc in first row, ch 3, skip next 2 rows, sc in next row, ch 3, sc in sp on Center of Strip, ch 3, sc in next row, ch 3, skip next 2 rows, sc in last row, ch 3; repeat from ★ 2 times **more** †; working across sts on Row 4, 2 sc in first dc, repeat from † to † once; join with slip st to first sc, finish off.

FRINGE

Holding 7 strands of Lt Green yarn together, each 18" long, add fringe in each ch-3 sp across short edges of Afghan *(Figs. 11a & b, page 144)*.

Design by Terry Kimbrough.

GARDEN PATCHWORK

Continued from page 24.

ONE SIDE JOINING

Rnd 3 (Joining rnd): Ch 3, 2 dc in same sp, ch 1, ★ 3 dc in next sp, ch 1, (3 dc, ch 2, 3 dc) in next sp, ch 1; repeat from ★ once **more**, (3 dc in next sp, ch 1) twice, holding Squares with **wrong** sides together, slip st in corresponding ch-2 sp on **previous Square**, ch 1, 3 dc in same sp on **new Square**, ch 1, slip st in next ch-1 sp on **previous Square**, 3 dc in next sp on **new Square**, ch 1, slip st in next ch-1 sp on **previous Square**, 3 dc in same sp as first dc on **new Square**, ch 1, slip st in next ch-2 sp on **previous Square**, ch 1; join with slip st to first dc, finish off.

TWO SIDE JOINING

Rnd 3 (Joining rnd)**:** Ch 3, 2 dc in same sp, ch 1, 3 dc in next sp, ch 1, (3 dc, ch 2, 3 dc) in next sp, ch 1, (3 dc in next sp, ch 1) twice, holding Squares with **wrong** sides together, slip st in

corresponding ch-2 sp on **previous Square**, ch 1, † 3 dc in same sp on **new Square**, ch 1, slip st in next ch-1 sp on **previous Square**, 3 dc in next sp on **new Square**, ch 1, slip st in next ch-1 sp on **previous Square** †, 3 dc in next sp on **new Square**, ch 1, (slip st in next ch-2 sp on **previous Square**, ch 1) twice, repeat from † to † once, 3 dc in same sp as first dc on **new Square**, ch 1, slip st in next ch-2 sp on **previous Square**, ch 1; join with slip st to first dc, finish off.

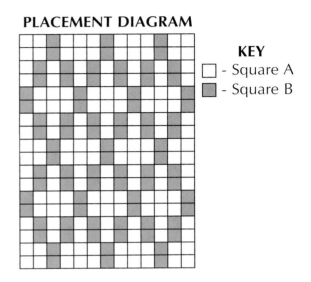

PLACEMENT DIAGRAM

KEY
☐ - Square A
▨ - Square B

EDGING

Rnd 1: With **right** side facing, join Off-White with slip st in any ch-2 sp; ch 3, 2 dc in same sp, ★ † ch 1, (3 dc in next ch-1 sp, ch 1) twice, [3 dc in next joining, ch 1, (3 dc in next ch-1 sp, ch 1) twice] across to next ch-2 sp †, (3 dc, ch 2, 3 dc) in ch-2 sp; repeat from ★ 2 times **more**, then repeat from † to † once, 3 dc in same sp as first dc, ch 1, sc in first dc to form last ch-2 sp.

Rnd 2: Ch 3, 2 dc in same sp, ★ † ch 1, (3 dc in next ch-1 sp, ch 1) across to next ch-2 sp †, (3 dc, ch 2, 3 dc) in ch-2 sp; repeat from ★ 2 times **more**, then repeat from † to † once, 3 dc in same sp as first dc, ch 2; join with slip st to first dc.

Rnd 3: Ch 1, sc in each dc and in each ch-1 sp around working 3 sc in each ch-2 sp; join with slip st to first sc, finish off.

Design by Judy Bolin.

43

STUNNING DAHLIAS

Continued from page 26.

skipping next 2 sc on same petal and first 2 sc on next petal and working in **both** petals, dc in next sc, ch 1, holding Flowers with **wrong** sides together, slip st in marked ch-3 sp on **previous Flower**, ch 1, dc in same st as last dc made on **new Flower**, ch 1, skip next 2 sc on new petal, sc in next sc, drop loop from hook, insert hook from **back** to **front** through **both** loops of next sc on **previous Flower**, hook dropped loop and draw through, ch 1, skipping next 2 sc on same petal and first 2 sc on next petal and working in **both** petals, dc in next sc, ch 1, slip st in next ch-3 sp on **previous Flower**, ch 1, dc in same st as last dc made on **new Flower**, ch 1; join with slip st to **both** loops of first sc, finish off.

BORDER

With White, ch 5, with **right** side of last Flower facing, slip st in second ch-3 sp before marker, ch 2, turn; skip next 2 chs of ch-5, dc in last 3 chs, ch 4 (**counts as first tr, now and throughout**), turn; † tr in next dc, dc in last dc, ch 2, slip st in next sc on Flower, ch 2, turn; dc in first dc, tr in last 2 tr, ch 4, turn; tr in next tr, dc in last dc, ch 2, slip st in next ch-3 sp on Flower, ch 2, turn; ★ dc in first dc, tr in last 2 tr, ch 4, turn; tr in next tr, dc in last dc, ch 2, slip st in next sc on Flower, ch 2, turn; dc in first dc, tr in last 2 tr, ch 4, turn; tr in next tr, dc in last dc, ch 2, slip st in next ch-3 sp on Flower, ch 2, turn; repeat from ★ once **more**, dc in first dc and in last 2 tr, ch 5, turn; dc in first 3 dc, ch 2, slip st in next sc on Flower, ch 2, turn; dc in first 3 dc, ch 5, turn; dc in first 3 dc, ♥ ch 2, slip st in next ch-3 sp on Flower, ch 2, turn; dc in first 3 dc, ch 5, turn; dc in first 3 dc, ch 2, decrease, ch 2, turn; dc in first 3 dc, ch 5, turn; dc in first 3 dc, ch 2, slip st in next ch-3 sp on Flower, ch 2, turn; dc in first 3 dc, ch 5, turn; dc in first 3 dc, ch 2, slip st in next sc on Flower, ch 2, turn; dc in first 3 dc, ch 5, turn; dc in first 3 dc ♥; repeat from ♥ to ♥ 12 times **more** †, ch 2, slip st in next ch-3 sp on Flower, ch 2, turn; dc in first 3 dc, ch 4, turn; repeat from † to † once, turn; working in free loops of beginning ch (*Fig. 3b, page 143*) **and** in dc just made, slip st in each st across, finish off.

REMAINING 6 STRIPS

Work 14 Flowers same as First Strip.

BORDER

With White, ch 5, with **right** side of last Flower facing, slip st in second ch-3 sp before marker, ch 2, turn; skip next 2 chs of ch-5, dc in last 3 chs, † ch 4, turn; tr in next dc, dc in last dc, ch 2, slip st in next sc on Flower, ch 2, turn; dc in first dc, tr in last 2 tr, ch 4, turn; tr in next tr, dc in last dc, ch 2, slip st in next ch-3 sp on Flower, ch 2, turn; [dc in first dc, tr in last 2 tr, ch 4, turn; tr in next tr, dc in last dc, ch 2, slip st in next sc on Flower, ch 2, turn; dc in first dc, tr in last 2 tr, ch 4, turn; tr in next tr, dc in last dc, ch 2, slip st in next ch-3 sp on Flower, ch 2, turn] twice, dc in first dc and in last 2 tr †, ch 5, turn; dc in first 3 dc, ch 2, slip st in next sc on Flower, ch 2, turn; dc in first 3 dc, ch 5, turn; dc in first 3 dc, ch 2, slip st in next ch-3 sp on Flower, ch 2, turn; dc in first 3 dc, ★ ch 5, turn; dc in first 3 dc, ch 2, decrease, ch 2, turn; dc in first 3 dc, ch 5, turn; dc in first 3 dc, ch 2, slip st in next ch-3 sp on Flower, ch 2, turn; dc in first 3 dc, ch 5, turn; dc in first 3 dc, ch 2, slip st in next sc on Flower, ch 2, turn; dc in first 3 dc, ch 5, turn; dc in first 3 dc, ch 2, slip st in next ch-3 sp on Flower, ch 2, turn; dc in first 3 dc; repeat from ★ 12 times **more**, then repeat from † to † once, ch 2, turn; holding Strips with **wrong** sides together, slip st in corresponding ch-5 sp on **previous Strip**, ch 2, dc in first 3 dc on **new Strip**, ch 2, slip st in next sc on Flower, ch 2, turn; dc in first 3 dc, ch 2, turn; slip st in next ch-5 sp on **previous Strip**, ch 2, dc in first 3 dc on **new Strip**, ♥ ch 2, slip st in next ch-3 sp on Flower, ch 2, turn; dc in first 3 dc, ch 2, turn; slip st in next ch-5 sp on **previous Strip**, ch 2, dc in first 3 dc on **new Strip**, ch 2, decrease, ch 2, turn; dc in first 3 dc, ch 2, turn; slip st in next ch-5 sp on **previous Strip**, ch 2, dc in first 3 dc on **new Strip**, ch 2, slip st in next ch-3 sp on Flower, ch 2, turn; dc in first 3 dc, ch 2, turn; slip st in next ch-5 sp on **previous Strip**, ch 2, dc in first 3 dc on **new Strip**, ch 2, slip st in next sc on Flower, ch 2, turn; dc in first 3 dc, ch 2, turn; slip st in next ch-5 sp on **previous Strip**, ch 2, dc in first 3 dc on **new Strip** ♥; repeat from ♥ to ♥ across, turn; working in free loops of beginning ch **and** in dc just made, slip st in each st across, finish off.

Design by Tammy Kreimeyer.

44

QUIET MOMENT

Continued from page 28.

ASSEMBLY

Using Placement Diagram as a guide, whipstitch Motifs together forming 6 horizontal strips of 7 Motifs each and 5 horizontal strips of 6 Motifs and 2 Half Motifs each *(Fig. 9a, page 144)*, beginning in center ch of first corner ch-3 and ending in center ch of next corner ch-3; then whipstitch strips together, beginning in first tr on Half Motif and in center ch of first corner ch-3 on Motif and ending in last tr on Half Motif and in center ch of last ch-3 on Motif.

PLACEMENT DIAGRAM

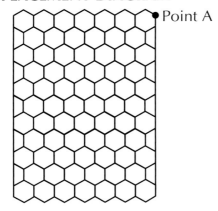 ● Point A

BORDER

Rnd 1: With **right** side facing, join yarn with sc in ch-3 sp at Point A *(see Joining With Sc, page 142)*; ch 1, sc in same sp, † ch 1, skip next tr, (sc in next tr, ch 1, skip next tr) 5 times, [(sc, ch 1) twice in next ch-3 sp, skip next tr, (sc in next tr, ch 1, skip next tr) 5 times, (sc in next sp, ch 1) twice, skip next tr, (sc in next tr, ch 1, skip next tr) 5 times] 6 times, [(sc, ch 1) twice in next ch-3 sp, skip next tr, (sc in next tr, ch 1, skip next tr) 5 times] twice, ★ sc in next sp, ch 1, skip next joining; working in end of rows on Half Motif, sc in next row, ch 1, hdc in top of next row, ch 1, sc in same row, ch 1, (sc, ch 1) twice in next row, hdc in next row, ch 1, hdc in ring, ch 1, hdc in next row, ch 1, (sc, ch 1) twice in next row, sc in next row, ch 1, hdc in top of same row, ch 1, sc in next row, ch 1, skip next joining, sc in next sp, ch 1, skip next tr, (sc in next tr, ch 1, skip next tr) 5 times; repeat from ★ 4 times **more** †, (sc, ch 1, sc) in next ch-3 sp, place marker around last ch-1 made for st placement, repeat from † to † once; join with slip st to first sc: 410 sts and 410 ch-1 sps.

Rnd 2: Ch 3 **(counts as first dc, now and throughout)**, 3 dc in next ch-1 sp, † dc in next sc, (dc in next ch-1 sp and in next sc) 6 times, 3 dc in next ch-1 sp, dc in next sc, ★ (dc in next ch-1 sp and in next sc) 5 times, work 3-dc decrease, dc in next sc, (dc in next ch-1 sp and in next sc) 5 times, 3 dc in next ch-1 sp, dc in next sc; repeat from ★ 5 times **more**, (dc in next ch-1 sp and in next sc) 6 times, 3 dc in next ch-1 sp †, dc in next sc, (dc in next ch-1 sp and in next st) across to marked ch-1 sp, 3 dc in marked ch-1 sp, remove marker and place marker around center dc of 3-dc group just made for st placement, repeat from † to † once, (dc in next st and in next ch-1 sp) across; join with slip st to first dc: 808 dc.

Rnd 3: Ch 3, dc in next dc, 3 dc in next dc, † dc in next 15 dc, 3 dc in next dc, ★ dc in next 11 dc, decrease, dc in next 11 dc, 3 dc in next dc; repeat from ★ 5 times **more**, dc in next 15 dc, 3 dc in next dc †, dc in each dc across to marked dc, 3 dc in marked dc, repeat from † to † once, dc in each dc across; join with slip st to first dc: 820 dc.

Rnd 4: Ch 2, skip next dc, ★ slip st in next dc, ch 2, skip next dc; repeat from ★ around; join with slip st to joining slip st, finish off.

Design by Anne Halliday.

FRESH AS A DAISY

Continued from page 30.

PLACEMENT DIAGRAM

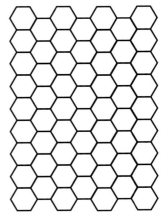

EDGING

With **right** side facing, join Green with slip st in any sc; ch 1, (slip st in next sc, ch 1) around; join with slip st to first slip st, finish off.

Design by Roberta Maier.

Come and sit a spell

Oh, the simple things in life ...
a leisurely walk, a cup of tea,
and taking time to relax and
"sit a spell" with old friends. We've
devoted this section to the special moments
that create our fondest memories.
You'll love our floral designs, stripes,
granny squares, and ripples —
all perfect for cuddling.

Spring Breezes

Finished Size: 55" x 64"

MATERIALS

Worsted Weight Yarn:
Lt Green - 48 ounces,
(1,360 grams, 3,290 yards)
Green - $^3/_4$ ounce, (20 grams, 50 yards)
Crochet hook, size I (5.50 mm) **or** size needed
for gauge
Yarn needle

GAUGE SWATCH: $4^1/_2$" square
Work same as Square.

STITCH GUIDE

> **TREBLE CROCHET** *(abbreviated tr)*
> YO twice, insert hook in sp indicated, YO and
> pull up a loop (4 loops on hook), (YO and
> draw through 2 loops on hook) 3 times.

SQUARE (Make 168)

With Lt Green, ch 4; join with slip st to form a
ring.

Rnd 1 (Right side)**:** Ch 5 **(counts as first tr plus
ch 1)**, (tr in ring, ch 1) 7 times; join with slip st to
first tr: 8 tr.

Note: Loop a short piece of yarn around any stitch
to mark Rnd 1 as **right** side.

Rnd 2: Ch 1, sc in same st, ch 5, (sc in next tr,
ch 5) around; join with slip st to first sc:
8 ch-5 sps.

Rnd 3: Ch 4 **(counts as first dc plus ch 1)**, (dc,
ch 1) twice in next ch-5 sp, ★ dc in next sc, ch 1,
(dc, ch 1) twice in next ch-5 sp; repeat from ★
around; join with slip st to first dc: 24 dc and
24 ch-1 sps.

Rnd 4: Ch 3 **(counts as first dc)**, ★ † dc in next
ch-1 sp and in next dc, (dc, ch 3, dc) in next
ch-1 sp, dc in next dc, dc in next ch-1 sp and in
next dc, hdc in next ch-1 sp, sc in next dc, sc in
next ch-1 sp and in next dc, hdc in next ch-1 sp †,
dc in next dc; repeat from ★ 2 times **more**, then
repeat from † to † once; join with slip st to first dc,
finish off: 52 sts and 4 ch-3 sps.

ASSEMBLY

With Lt Green and working through **both** loops of
both pieces, whipstitch Squares together forming
12 vertical strips of 14 Squares each **(Fig. 9a,
page 144)**, beginning in center ch of first corner
and ending in center ch of next corner; then
whipstitch strips together in same manner.

EDGING

Rnd 1: With **right** side facing, join Green with sc
in lower right corner ch-3 sp **(see Joining With Sc,
page 142)**; 2 sc in same sp, ★ † skip next dc, sc in
next 12 sts, (sc in next 2 sps and in next 13 sts)
across to next corner ch-3 sp †, 3 sc in corner
ch-3 sp; repeat from ★ 2 times **more**, then repeat
from † to † once; join with slip st to first sc,
finish off: 780 sc.

Rnd 2: With **right** side facing, join Lt Green with
slip st in center sc of any corner 3-sc group; ch 5,
slip st in same st, ch 5, ★ † skip next 2 sc, (slip st
in next sc, ch 5, skip next 2 sc) across to center sc
of next corner 3-sc group †, (slip st, ch 5) twice in
center sc; repeat from ★ 2 times **more**, then repeat
from † to † once; join with slip st to first slip st,
finish off.

Design by Sue Galucki.

Colorful Mosaic

Finished Size: 47¹/₂" x 65"

MATERIALS
Worsted Weight Yarn:
 Blue - 28 ounces, (800 grams, 1,580 yards)
 Scraps - 39 ounces,
  (1,110 grams, 2,205 yards) **total**
 Note: We used 9 different colors.
Crochet hook, size I (5.50 mm) **or** size needed
 for gauge
Yarn needle

GAUGE SWATCH: 3¹/₂" square
Work same as Square.

STITCH GUIDE

> **TREBLE CROCHET *(abbreviated tr)***
> YO twice, insert hook in st or sp indicated, YO
> and pull up a loop (4 loops on hook), (YO and
> draw through 2 loops on hook) 3 times.

SQUARE (Make 234)
Rnd 1: With color desired, ch 2, 8 sc in second ch
from hook; join with slip st to first sc.

Rnd 2: Ch 1, (sc, ch 3, sc) in same st, tr in next sc,
★ (sc, ch 3, sc) in next sc, tr in next sc; repeat
from ★ 2 times **more**; join with slip st to first sc:
12 sts and 4 ch-3 sps.

Rnd 3 (Right side): Ch 1, **turn**; sc in next tr, dc in
next sc, (sc, ch 3, sc) in next corner ch-3 sp, ★ dc
in next sc, sc in next tr, dc in next sc, (sc, ch 3, sc)
in next corner ch-3 sp; repeat from ★ 2 times
more, dc in last sc; join with slip st to first sc:
20 sts and 4 ch-3 sps.

Note: Loop a short piece of yarn around any stitch
to mark Rnd 3 as **right** side.

Rnd 4: Ch 1, turn; sc in next dc, tr in next sc, (sc,
ch 3, sc) in next corner ch-3 sp, tr in next sc, ★ (sc
in next dc, tr in next sc) twice, (sc, ch 3, sc) in
next corner ch-3 sp, tr in next sc; repeat from ★
2 times **more**, sc in next dc, tr in last sc; join with
slip st to first sc, finish off: 28 sts and 4 ch-3 sps.

Rnd 5: With **right** side facing, join Blue with sc in
any corner ch-3 sp *(see Joining With Sc,
page 142)*; ch 3, sc in same sp, dc in next sc, (sc
in next tr, dc in next sc) 3 times, ★ (sc, ch 3, sc) in
next corner ch-3 sp, dc in next sc, (sc in next tr, dc
in next sc) 3 times; repeat from ★ 2 times **more**;
join with slip st to first sc, finish off: 36 sts and
4 ch-3 sps.

ASSEMBLY
With Blue, whipstitch Squares together forming
13 vertical strips of 18 Squares each *(Fig. 9a,
page 144)*, beginning in center ch of first corner
ch-3 and ending in center ch of next corner ch-3;
then whipstitch strips together in same manner.

EDGING
Rnd 1: With **wrong** side facing, join Blue with sc
in any corner ch-3 sp; ch 3, sc in same sp, ★ ✝ dc
in next sc, (sc in next dc, dc in next sc) 4 times,
[sc in next sp, dc in next joining, sc in next sp, dc
in next sc, (sc in next dc, dc in next sc) 4 times]
across to next corner ch-3 sp ✝, (sc, ch 3, sc) in
corner ch-3 sp; repeat from ★ 2 times **more**, then
repeat from ✝ to ✝ once; join with slip st to first sc:
740 sts and 4 ch-3 sps.

Rnd 2: Ch 1, turn; ★ (sc in next dc, dc in next sc)
across to next corner ch-3 sp, (sc, ch 3, sc) in
corner ch-3 sp, dc in next sc; repeat from ★
around; join with slip st to first sc: 748 sts and
4 ch-3 sps.

Rnd 3: Ch 1, turn; sc in next dc, ch 1, skip next
sc, (sc, ch 3, sc) in next corner ch-3 sp, ch 1,
★ skip next sc, (sc in next dc, ch 1, skip next sc)
across to next corner ch-3 sp, (sc, ch 3, sc) in
corner ch-3 sp, ch 1; repeat from ★ 2 times **more**,
skip next sc, (sc in next dc, ch 1, skip next sc)
across; join with slip st to first sc: 380 sps.

Rnd 4: Ch 1, turn; ★ (slip st in next ch-1 sp, ch 1)
across to next corner ch-3 sp, (slip st, ch 2, slip st)
in corner ch-3 sp, ch 1; repeat from ★ 3 times
more, slip st in last ch-1 sp, ch 1; join with slip st
to first slip st, finish off.

Design by Anne Halliday.

THIS BRILLIANT, TEXTURED THROW IS A MOSAIC OF BEAUTIFUL COLORS. GATHER YOUR SCRAPS TO MAKE THE SQUARES IN A VARIETY OF HUES, THEN USE A SINGLE STRONG COLOR TO JOIN THEM.

Finished Size: 49$\frac{1}{2}$" x 64$\frac{1}{2}$"

MATERIALS

Worsted Weight Yarn:
Lavender - 20 ounces, (570 grams, 1,305 yards)
Ecru - 12 ounces, (340 grams, 780 yards)
Lt Green - 11 ounces,
(310 grams, 715 yards)
Crochet hook, size H (5.00 mm) **or** size needed for gauge

GAUGE: Each Strip = 5$\frac{1}{2}$" wide

Gauge Swatch: 2$\frac{3}{4}$" diameter
Work same as First Flower.

STITCH GUIDE

DECREASE
YO, insert hook in same st or sp, YO and pull up a loop, YO and draw through 2 loops on hook, for second leg, YO, insert hook in st or sp indicated, YO and pull up a loop, YO and draw through 2 loops on hook, YO and draw through all 3 loops on hook.

CLUSTER (uses first 3 dc)
Ch 2, **turn**; skip first dc, ★ YO, insert hook in **next** dc, YO and pull up a loop, YO and draw through 2 loops on hook; repeat from ★ once **more**, YO and draw through all 3 loops on hook.

DOUBLE CLUSTER
YO, insert hook in same st, YO and pull up a loop, YO and draw through 2 loops on hook, YO twice, insert hook in next joining, YO and pull up a loop, (YO and draw through 2 loops on hook) twice, YO and draw through all 3 loops on hook, YO twice, insert hook in same st, YO and pull up a loop, (YO and draw through 2 loops on hook) twice, YO, insert hook at top of next petal, YO and pull up a loop, YO and draw through 2 loops on hook, YO and draw through all 3 loops on hook.

FIRST STRIP
FIRST FLOWER
With Lavender, ch 6; join with slip st to form a ring.

Rnd 1: Ch 3 **(counts as first dc, now and throughout)**, 3 dc in ring, place marker around last dc made to mark **right** side, work Cluster, ch 3, **turn**; (4 dc in ring, work Cluster, ch 3, **turn**) twice, place marker in back ridge of third ch from hook for joining placement **(Fig. 1, page 143)**, (4 dc in ring, work Cluster, ch 3, **turn**) 3 times; join with slip st to first dc, finish off: 6 petals.

REMAINING 21 FLOWERS
With Lavender, ch 6; join with slip st to form a ring.

Rnd 1 (Joining rnd)**:** Ch 3, 3 dc in ring, work Cluster, ch 3, **turn**; (4 dc in ring, work Cluster, ch 3, **turn**) twice, place marker in back ridge of third ch from hook for joining placement, (4 dc in ring, work Cluster, ch 3, **turn**) twice, 4 dc in ring, work Cluster, holding Flowers with **right** side of **new Flower** and **wrong** side of **previous Flower** together, slip st in marked ch on **previous Flower**, ch 3, **turn**; join with slip st to first dc on **new Flower**, finish off: 6 petals.

BORDER
Rnd 1: With **right** side facing, join Lt Green with slip st in marked ch on last Flower; ch 8, (2 dc, ch 5, dc) in same st, † [decrease working second leg at top of next petal, (dc, ch 5, dc) in same st] twice, work Double Cluster, ★ (dc, ch 5, dc) in same st, decrease working second leg at top of next petal, (dc, ch 5, dc) in same st, work Double Cluster; repeat from ★ 19 times **more**, [(dc, ch 5, dc) in same st, decrease working second leg at top of next petal] twice †, (dc, ch 5, 2 dc, ch 5, dc) in same st, repeat from † to † once working second leg of last decrease in same st as beginning ch-8; join with slip st to third ch of beginning ch-8, finish off: 92 ch-5 sps.

Continued on page 75.

Eye-catching Posies

Finished Size: 44" x 66"

MATERIALS
Worsted Weight Yarn:
    Black - 47 ounces, (1,330 grams, 2,655 yards)
    Scraps - 24 ounces,
       (680 grams, 1,355 yards) **total**
    Note: We used 6 different colors.
    Each Square requires 55 yards.
Crochet hook, size Q (15.00 mm)

Afghan is worked holding three strands of yarn together.

GAUGE: Each Square = 11"

Gauge Swatch: 3" square
Work same as First Square through Rnd 1.

FIRST SQUARE

With color desired, ch 3; join with slip st to form a ring.

Rnd 1 (Right side)**:** Ch 2 **(counts as first hdc)**, 2 hdc in ring, ch 1, (3 hdc in ring, ch 1) 3 times; join with slip st to first hdc, finish off: 12 hdc and 4 ch-1 sps.

Note: Loop a short piece of yarn around any stitch to mark Rnd 1 as **right** side.

Rnd 2: With **right** side facing, join color desired with sc in center hdc of any 3-hdc group **(see Joining With Sc, page 142)**; skip next hdc, 9 dc in next ch-1 sp, skip next hdc, ★ sc in next hdc, skip next hdc, 9 dc in next ch-1 sp, skip next hdc; repeat from ★ 2 times **more**; join with slip st to first sc, finish off: 40 sts.

Rnd 3: With **right** side facing, join Black with slip st in any sc; ch 3, hdc in same st, ch 2, skip next 3 dc, sc in next dc, ch 2, skip next dc, sc in next dc, ch 2, skip next 3 dc, ★ (hdc, ch 1, hdc) in next sc, ch 2, skip next 3 dc, sc in next dc, ch 2, skip next dc, sc in next dc, ch 2, skip next 3 dc; repeat from ★ 2 times **more**; join with slip st to second ch of beginning ch-3, do **not** finish off: 16 sps.

Rnd 4: Slip st in first ch-1 sp, ch 3, 3 dc in next ch-2 sp, (3 dc, ch 3, 3 dc) in next ch-2 sp, 3 dc in next ch-2 sp, ★ dc in next ch-1 sp, 3 dc in next ch-2 sp, (3 dc, ch 3, 3 dc) in next ch-2 sp, 3 dc in next ch-2 sp; repeat from ★ 2 times **more**; join with slip st to top of beginning ch-3: 52 sts and 4 ch-3 sps.

Rnd 5: Slip st in next dc, ch 1, sc in same st, ch 2, skip next dc, (sc in next dc, ch 2, skip next dc) twice, (sc, ch 3, sc) in next corner ch-3 sp, ch 2, ★ skip next dc, (sc in next dc, ch 2, skip next dc) 6 times, (sc, ch 3, sc) in next corner ch-3 sp, ch 2; repeat from ★ 2 times **more**, skip next dc, (sc in next dc, ch 2, skip next st) 3 times; join with slip st to first sc, finish off: 32 sps.

ADDITIONAL SQUARES

The method used to connect the Squares is a no-sew joining also known as "join-as-you-go". After the First Square is made, each remaining Square is worked through Rnd 4, then crocheted together as Rnd 5 is worked.

Work same as First Square through Rnd 4: 52 sts and 4 ch-3 sps.

Rnd 5 (Joining rnd)**:** Work One or Two Side Joining **(Fig. 10, page 144)**, arranging Squares into 4 vertical strips of 6 Squares each.

When working into a corner sp that has been previously joined, work into joining ch.

ONE SIDE JOINING

Rnd 5 (Joining rnd)**:** Slip st in next dc, ch 1, sc in same st, ch 2, skip next dc, (sc in next dc, ch 2, skip next dc) twice, ★ (sc, ch 3, sc) in next corner ch-3 sp, ch 2, skip next dc, (sc in next dc, ch 2, skip next dc) 6 times; repeat from ★ once **more**, sc in next corner ch-3 sp, ch 1, holding Squares with **wrong** sides together, drop loop from hook, insert hook from **back** to **front** in corresponding corner ch-3 sp on **previous Square**, hook dropped loop and pull through, ch 2, sc in same sp on **new Square**, ch 1, drop loop from hook, insert hook from **back** to **front** in next ch-2 sp on **previous Square**, hook dropped loop and pull through,

Continued on page 75.

PRETTY POSIES POSITIVELY GLOW AGAINST A
BACKDROP OF BLACK ON THIS EYE-CATCHING
THROW. SINGLE AND HALF DOUBLE CROCHET
STITCHES WORKED IN TRIPLE STRANDS
CREATE THIS CASUAL WRAP.

Pansy Delight

Finished Size: 46" x 64"

MATERIALS

Worsted Weight Yarn:

Ecru - $25^3/_4$ ounces, (730 grams, 1,765 yards)

Green - $11^1/_2$ ounces, (330 grams, 790 yards)

Lavender - $9^1/_2$ ounces, (270 grams, 650 yards)

Crochet hook, size H (5.00 mm) **or** size needed for gauge

Yarn needle

GAUGE: Each Square = $3^3/_4$"

Each Rectangle = $3^3/_4$"w x 11"h

Gauge Swatch: $2^1/_2$" square
Work same as Square through Rnd 3.

STITCH GUIDE

CLUSTER (uses one ch)
YO, insert hook in third ch from hook, YO and pull up a loop, YO and draw through 2 loops on hook, ★ YO, insert hook in **same** st, YO and pull up a loop, YO and draw through 2 loops on hook; repeat from ★ once **more**, YO and draw through all 4 loops on hook.

DECREASE (uses 2 sps)
YO, insert hook in same sp, YO and pull up a loop, YO and draw through 2 loops on hook, YO, insert hook in next sp, YO and pull up a loop, YO and draw through 2 loops on hook, YO and draw through all 3 loops on hook.

SQUARE (Make 60)

With Lavender, ch 4; join with slip st to form a ring.

Rnd 1 (Right side)**:** Ch 1, (sc in ring, ch 2) 4 times; join with slip st to first sc: 4 ch-2 sps.

Note: Loop a short piece of yarn around any stitch to mark Rnd 1 as **right** side.

Rnd 2: (Sc, 4 hdc, sc, slip st) in each ch-2 sp around; do **not** join: 4 petals.

Rnd 3: Skip first sc, sc in next hdc, (ch 3, sc in next st) 4 times, ★ skip next 2 sts, sc in next hdc, (ch 3, sc in next st) 4 times; repeat from ★ 2 times **more**, slip st in next slip st; do **not** join: 16 ch-3 sps.

Rnd 4: Ch 3, working **behind** petals and in ch-2 sps on Rnd 1 *(Fig. 6, page 143)*, ★ skip first 3 sts of **next** petal, sc in sp **before** next hdc *(Fig. 5, page 143)*, ch 5; repeat from ★ around; join with slip st to first sc, finish off: 4 ch-5 sps.

Rnd 5: With **right** side facing and working **behind** petals, join Green with slip st in any ch-5 sp; ch 3 **(counts as first dc, now and throughout)**, (2 dc, ch 3, 3 dc) in same sp, ch 1, ★ (3 dc, ch 3, 3 dc) in next ch-5 sp, ch 1; repeat from ★ 2 times **more**; join with slip st to first dc, finish off: 24 dc and 8 sps.

Rnd 6: With **right** side facing, join Ecru with slip st in any corner ch-3 sp; ch 3, (2 dc, ch 3, 3 dc) in same sp, ch 1, 3 dc in next ch-1 sp, ch 1, ★ (3 dc, ch 3, 3 dc) in next corner ch-3 sp, ch 1, 3 dc in next ch-1 sp, ch 1; repeat from ★ 2 times **more**; join with slip st to first dc, finish off: 12 sps.

RECTANGLE (Make 48)

Foundation Row (Wrong side)**:** With Lavender, (ch 4, work Cluster) 7 times, ch 1; finish off.

Note: Mark **back** of any Cluster on Foundation Row as **right** side.

Rnd 1: With **right** side facing, join Green with slip st in first ch; ch 3, [2 dc, (ch 3, 3 dc) twice] in same ch, ch 1, skip next Cluster, (3 dc in next ch, ch 1, skip next Cluster) across to last ch, [3 dc, (ch 3, 3 dc) twice] in last ch, ch 1; working in free loops of chs *(Fig. 3b, page 143)*, skip next Cluster, (3 dc in next ch, ch 1, skip next Cluster) across; join with slip st to first dc, finish off: 18 sps.

Continued to page 76.

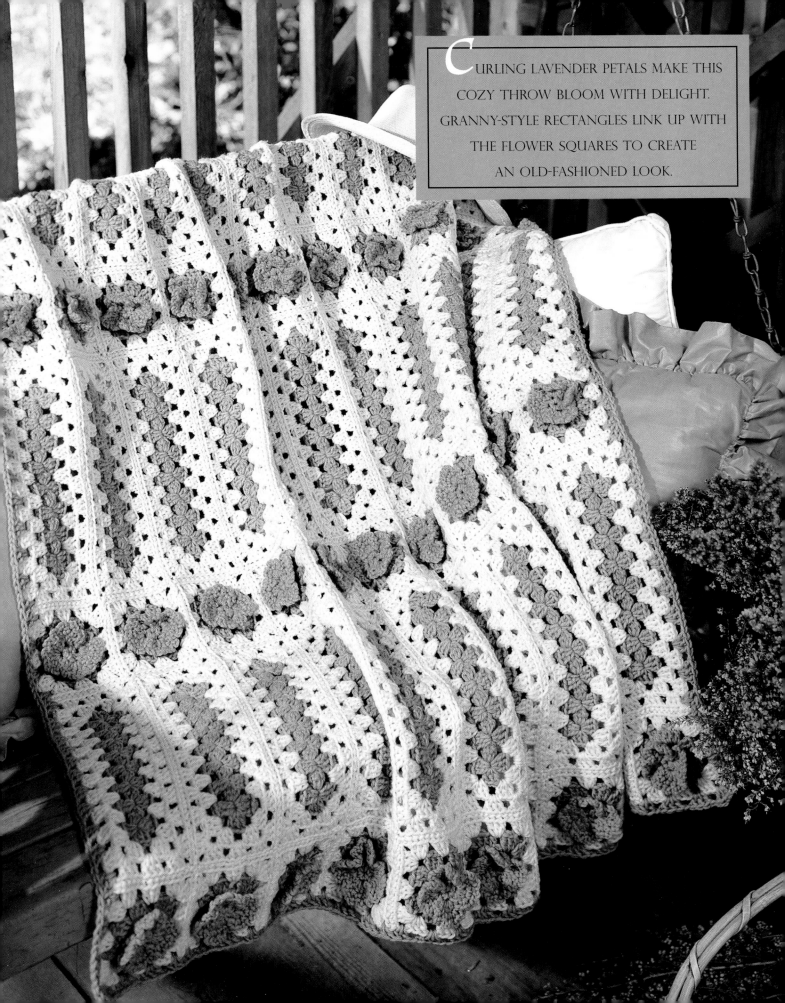

CURLING LAVENDER PETALS MAKE THIS
COZY THROW BLOOM WITH DELIGHT.
GRANNY-STYLE RECTANGLES LINK UP WITH
THE FLOWER SQUARES TO CREATE
AN OLD-FASHIONED LOOK.

Rosy Dream

Finished Size: 51¹/₂" x 67¹/₂"

MATERIALS

Worsted Weight Yarn:
  Ecru - 31 ounces, (880 grams, 2,125 yards)
  Green - 14 ounces, (400 grams, 960 yards)
  Rose - 8¹/₂ ounces, (240 grams, 585 yards)
Crochet hook, size H (5.00 mm) **or** size needed
  for gauge
Yarn needle

GAUGE: Each Square = 8"

Gauge Swatch: 4" square
Work same as Square through Rnd 2.

STITCH GUIDE

LONG DOUBLE CROCHET
  (abbreviated LDC)
YO, insert hook in sp indicated, YO and pull up
a loop even with loop on hook (3 loops on
hook), (YO and draw through 2 loops on hook)
twice.

DECREASE
YO, working in **front** of previous rnd and in sps
one rnd **below (Fig. 6, page 143)**, insert hook in
same sp after last 3-dc group just worked into,
YO and pull up a loop even with loop on hook,
YO and draw through 2 loops on hook, YO,
insert hook in next ch-5 sp **before** next dc group,
YO and pull up a loop even with loop on hook,
YO and draw through 2 loops on hook, YO and
draw through all 3 loops on hook.

CLUSTER
Ch 3, YO, insert hook in third ch from hook,
YO and pull up a loop, YO and draw through
2 loops on hook, YO, insert hook in same ch,
YO and pull up a loop, YO and draw through
2 loops on hook, YO and draw through all
3 loops on hook.

SQUARE (Make 48)

With Rose, ch 8; join with slip st to form a ring.

Rnd 1 (Right side)**:** Ch 3 **(counts as first dc, now
and throughout)**, 2 dc in ring, place marker
around last dc made to mark **right** side, ch 3, **turn**;
skip first dc, dc in next dc **(first Petal made)**, ch 3,
turn; ★ 3 dc in ring, ch 3, **turn**; skip first dc, dc in
next dc **(Petal made)**, ch 3, **turn**; repeat from **★**
10 times **more**; join with slip st to first dc,
finish off: 12 Petals.

Note: Loop a short piece of yarn around any stitch
to mark Rnd 1 as **right** side.

Rnd 2: With **right** side facing and working in
ch-3 sps between Petals, join Green with slip st in
any ch-3 sp; ch 3, 2 dc in same sp, ch 1, 3 dc in
next ch-3 sp, ch 1, (dc, ch 3, dc) in next ch-3 sp,
ch 1, **★** (3 dc in next ch-3 sp, ch 1) twice, (dc,
ch 3, dc) in next ch-3 sp, ch 1; repeat from **★**
2 times **more**; join with slip st to first dc, finish off:
32 dc and 16 sps.

Rnd 3: With **right** side facing, join Ecru with slip st
in any corner ch-3 sp; ch 3, 2 dc in same sp, dc in
next dc, 2 dc in next ch-1 sp, ch 3, sc in next
ch-1 sp, ch 3, 2 dc in next ch-1 sp, dc in next dc,
★ (3 dc, ch 3, 3 dc) in next corner ch-3 sp, dc in
next dc, 2 dc in next ch-1 sp, ch 3, sc in next
ch-1 sp, ch 3, 2 dc in next ch-1 sp, dc in next dc;
repeat from **★** 2 times **more**, 3 dc in same sp as
first dc, ch 1, hdc in first dc to form last corner
ch-3 sp; do **not** finish off: 52 sts and 12 ch-3 sps.

Rnd 4: Ch 1, sc in last corner ch-3 sp made, ch 5,
skip next 3 dc, sc in sp **before** next dc **(Fig. 5,
page 143)**, ch 5, (sc in next ch-3 sp, ch 5) twice,
skip next 3 dc, sc in sp **before** next dc, ch 5,
★ (sc, ch 5) twice in next corner ch-3 sp, skip next
3 dc, sc in sp **before** next dc, ch 5, (sc in next
ch-3 sp, ch 5) twice, skip next 3 dc, sc in sp
before next dc, ch 5; repeat from **★** 2 times **more**,
sc in same sp as first sc, ch 5; join with slip st to
first sc, finish off: 24 ch-5 sps.

Continued on page 77.

Finished Size: 44" x 58"

MATERIALS

Worsted Weight Yarn:

Off-White - 23$\frac{1}{2}$ ounces,
(670 grams, 1,330 yards)

Green - 8 ounces, (230 grams, 450 yards)

Scraps - 16 ounces,
(450 grams, 905 yards) **total**

Note: We used 3 different colors.

Crochet hook, size G (4.00 mm) **or** size needed for gauge

GAUGE: Each Square = 7"

Gauge Swatch: 3" diameter
Work same as First Square through Rnd 2.

FIRST SQUARE

With Off-White, ch 4; join with slip st to form a ring.

Rnd 1 (Right side)**:** Ch 6, (dc in ring, ch 3) 7 times; join with slip st to third ch of beginning ch-6: 8 sts and 8 ch-3 sps.

Note: Loop a short piece of yarn around any stitch to mark Rnd 1 as **right** side.

Rnd 2: Ch 1, sc in same st, 3 dc in next ch-3 sp, (sc in next dc, 3 dc in next ch-3 sp) around; join with slip st to first sc, finish off: 32 sts.

Rnd 3: With **right** side facing, join color desired with dc in any sc **(see Joining With Dc, page 142)**; 4 dc in same st, skip next dc, sc in next dc, skip next dc, ★ 5 dc in next sc, skip next dc, sc in next dc, skip next dc; repeat from ★ around; join with slip st to first dc, finish off: 48 sts.

Rnd 4: With **right** side facing, join Green with dc in center dc of any 5-dc group; (2 dc, ch 3, 3 dc) in same st, ch 1, skip next 2 dc, 3 dc in next sc, ch 1, skip next 2 dc, sc in next dc, ch 1, skip next 2 dc, 3 dc in next sc, ch 1, skip next 2 dc, ★ (3 dc, ch 3, 3 dc) in next dc, ch 1, skip next 2 dc, 3 dc in next sc, ch 1, skip next 2 dc, sc in next dc, ch 1, skip next 2 dc, 3 dc in next sc,

ch 1, skip next 2 dc; repeat from ★ 2 times **more**; join with slip st to first dc, finish off: 52 sts and 20 sps.

Rnd 5: With **right** side facing, join Off-White with sc in any ch **(see Joining With Sc, page 142)**; sc in each ch and in Back Loop Only of each st around **(Fig. 2, page 143)** working 3 sc in center ch of each corner ch-3; join with slip st to **both** loops of first sc, finish off: 88 sc.

Rnd 6: With **right** side facing and working in both loops, join color desired with dc in center sc of any corner 3-sc group; 2 dc in same st, dc in each sc around working 3 dc in center sc of each corner 3-sc group; join with slip st to first dc, finish off: 96 dc.

Rnd 7: With **right** side facing and working in Back Loops Only, join Off-White with sc in center dc of any corner 3-dc group; 2 sc in same st, sc in each dc around working 3 sc in center dc of each corner 3-dc group; join with slip st to **both** loops of first sc, do **not** finish off: 104 sc.

Rnd 8: Slip st in both loops of next sc, ch 1, (sc, ch 3) twice in same st, skip next sc, (sc in next sc, ch 3, skip next sc) across to center sc of next corner 3-sc group, ★ (sc, ch 3) twice in center sc, skip next sc, (sc in next sc, ch 3, skip next sc) across to center sc of next corner 3-sc group; repeat from ★ 2 times **more**; join with slip st to first sc, finish off: 56 ch-3 sps.

REMAINING 47 SQUARES

The method used to connect the Squares is a no-sew joining also known as "join-as-you-go". After the First Square is made, each remaining Square is worked through Rnd 7, then crocheted together as Rnd 8 is worked.

Work same as First Square through Rnd 7: 104 sc.

Rnd 8 (Joining rnd)**:** Work One or Two Side Joining **(Fig. 10, page 144)**, arranging Squares into 6 vertical strips of 8 Squares each.

When working into a corner sp that has been previously joined, work into joining sc.

Continued on page 78.

Teatime Tulips

Finished Size: 48" x 66"

MATERIALS
Worsted Weight Yarn:
Ecru - 19 ounces, (540 grams, 1,240 yards)
Lt Green - 18 ounces,
(510 grams, 1,175 yards)
Pink - 12 ounces, (340 grams, 780 yards)
Crochet hook, size H (5.00 mm) **or** size needed
for gauge

GAUGE: 10 sc = 3"
Each Strip = 4" wide

Gauge Swatch: 3" wide
Ch 11 **loosely.**
Row 1: Sc in second ch from hook and in each ch
across: 10 sc.
Rows 2-5: Ch 1, turn; sc in each sc across.
Finish off.

STITCH GUIDE

TREBLE CROCHET (abbreviated tr)
YO twice, insert hook in st indicated, YO and
pull up a loop (4 loops on hook), (YO and
draw through 2 loops on hook) 3 times.

LONG SINGLE CROCHET (abbreviated LSC)
Insert hook in sp indicated, YO and pull up a
loop **even** with last st made, YO and draw
through both loops on hook.

CLUSTER
★ YO twice, insert hook in st indicated, YO
and pull up a loop, (YO and draw through
2 loops on hook) twice; repeat from ★ once
more, YO and draw through all 3 loops on
hook.

SPLIT CLUSTER
First Leg: ★ YO twice, insert hook in **same** st,
YO and pull up a loop, (YO and draw through
2 loops on hook) twice; repeat from ★ once
more (3 loops remaining on hook).

Second Leg: ★ YO twice, insert hook in sc
indicated, YO and pull up a loop, (YO and
draw through 2 loops on hook) twice; repeat
from ★ once **more**, YO and draw through all
5 loops on hook.

FRONT POST CLUSTER
(abbreviated FP Cluster)
★ YO, insert hook from **front** to **back** around
post of tr indicated **(Fig. 4, page 143)**, YO and
pull up a loop, YO and draw through 2 loops on
hook; repeat from ★ 2 times **more**, YO and draw
through all 4 loops on hook.

FIRST STRIP
With Ecru, ch 201 **loosely.**

Rnd 1 (Right side): 2 Sc in second ch from hook,
sc in each ch across to last ch, 3 sc in last ch;
working in free loops of beginning ch **(Fig. 3b,
page 143)**, sc in next 199 chs; join with slip st to
first sc, finish off: 402 sc.

Note: Loop a short piece of yarn around any stitch
to mark Rnd 1 as **right** side.

Rnd 2: With **right** side facing, join Lt Green with
slip st in same st as joining; ch 7 **(counts as first tr
plus ch 3)**, (work Cluster, ch 3, tr) in same st,
† ch 3, work First Leg of Split Cluster, skip next
2 sc, work Second Leg of Split Cluster in next sc,
ch 3, tr in same st, ch 3, ★ work First Leg of
Split Cluster, skip next 4 sc, work Second Leg of
Split Cluster in next sc, ch 3, tr in same st, ch 3;
repeat from ★ 38 times **more**, work First Leg of
Split Cluster, skip next 2 sc †, work Second Leg of
Split Cluster in next sc, ch 3, (tr, ch 3, work
Cluster, ch 3, tr) in same st, repeat from † to †
once, work Second Leg of Split Cluster in same st
as first tr, ch 3; join with slip st to first tr, finish off:
84 tr and 168 ch-3 sps.

Rnd 3: With **right** side facing, join Pink with sc in
first ch-3 sp **(see Joining With Sc, page 142)**;
† ch 7, sc in next ch-3 sp, work FP Cluster around
next tr, ★ sc in next ch-3 sp, ch 5, sc in next
ch-3 sp, work FP Cluster around next tr; repeat
from ★ 40 times **more** †, sc in next ch-3 sp, repeat
from † to † once; join with slip st to first sc,
finish off: 84 FP Clusters.

Continued on page 78.

Finished Size: 50" x 66"

MATERIALS

Worsted Weight Yarn:
  White - 33 ounces, (940 grams, 1,865 yards)
  Green - 21 ounces, (600 grams, 1,190 yards)
  Blue - 2 ounces, (60 grams, 115 yards)
  Yellow - 2 ounces, (60 grams, 115 yards)
  Rose - 2 ounces, (60 grams, 115 yards)
  Purple - 2 ounces, (60 grams, 115 yards)
Crochet hook, size I (5.50 mm) **or** size needed
  for gauge
Yarn needle

GAUGE: Each Square = 8"

Gauge Swatch: $2^{3}/4$" diameter
Work same as Flower through Rnd 2.

STITCH GUIDE

> **TREBLE CROCHET (abbreviated tr)**
> YO twice, insert hook in st indicated, YO and
> pull up a loop (4 loops on hook), (YO and
> draw through 2 loops on hook) 3 times.

SQUARE (Make 48)
FLOWER

Make 12 Flowers **each** in the following colors:
Blue, Yellow, Rose, and Purple.

With color indicated, ch 5; join with slip st to form
a ring.

Rnd 1 (Right side)**:** Ch 3 **(counts as first dc, now
and throughout)**, 2 dc in ring, ch 1, (3 dc in ring,
ch 1) 4 times; join with slip st to first dc: 15 dc
and 5 ch-1 sps.

Note: Loop a short piece of yarn around any stitch
to mark Rnd 1 as **right** side.

Rnd 2: Ch 2 **(counts as first hdc)**, dc in next dc,
hdc in next dc, ch 2, ★ hdc in next dc, dc in next
dc, hdc in next dc, ch 2; repeat from ★ around;
join with slip st to first hdc: 15 sts and 5 ch-2 sps.

Rnd 3: Ch 3, working in Front Loops Only **(Fig. 2,
page 143)**, dc in same st, 2 tr in next dc, 2 dc in
next hdc, working **around** next ch-2 **(Fig. 6,
page 143)**, sc in ch one rnd **below** (petal made),
★ 2 dc in next hdc, 2 tr in next dc, 2 dc in next
hdc, working **around** next ch-2, sc in ch one rnd
below (petal made); repeat from ★ around; join
with slip st to first dc, finish off: 5 petals.

LEAVES

Rnd 1: With **right** side facing, working **behind**
petals and in free loops on Rnds 1 and 2 **(Fig. 3a,
page 143)**, join Green with slip st in any ch on
Rnd 1; ch 7, (2 tr, ch 4, slip st) in fifth ch from
hook, slip st in next 3 sts on Rnd 2, dc in next ch
on Rnd 1, (slip st, ch 4, 2 tr, ch 4, slip st) in next st
on Rnd 2, slip st in next 2 sts, dc in next ch on
Rnd 1, slip st in next st on Rnd 2, (slip st, ch 4,
2 tr, ch 4, slip st) in next st, slip st in next st, dc in
next ch on Rnd 1, slip st in next 2 sts on Rnd 2,
(slip st, ch 4, 2 tr, ch 4, slip st) in next st, dc in
next ch on Rnd 1, slip st in last 3 sts on Rnd 2;
join with slip st to third ch of beginning ch-7.

Rnd 2: Ch 1, ★ 4 sc in next ch-4 sp, skip next tr,
working in both loops, 2 sc in next tr, 4 sc in next
ch-4 sp, skip next slip st, sc in next 4 sts; repeat
from ★ around; join with slip st to first sc,
finish off: 56 sc.

BORDER

Rnd 1: With **right** side facing, join White with sc
in second sc of 2-sc group at tip of any Leaf **(see
Joining With Sc, page 142)**; sc in next 2 sc, hdc in
next sc, dc in next 6 sc, hdc in next sc, sc in next
3 sc, ch 2, ★ sc in next 3 sc, hdc in next sc, dc in
next 6 sc, hdc in next sc, sc in next 3 sc, ch 2;
repeat from ★ 2 times **more**; join with slip st to
first sc: 56 sts and 4 ch-2 sps.

Rnd 2: Ch 1, sc in same st and in each st across to
next corner ch-2 sp, 2 sc in corner ch-2 sp, (sc in
each st across to next corner ch-2 sp, 2 sc in
corner ch-2 sp) around; join with slip st to first sc,
finish off: 64 sc.

Continued on page 79.

Finished Size: 49" x 61"

MATERIALS

Worsted Weight Yarn:
45 ounces, (1,280 grams, 2,955 yards)
Crochet hook, size I (5.50 mm) **or** size needed for gauge
Yarn needle

GAUGE: Each Strip = 4³/₄" wide

Gauge Swatch: 3¹/₄"w x 3"h
Work same as Strip Center through Row 4.

STITCH GUIDE

> **CLUSTER** (uses next 3 dc)
> ★ YO, insert hook in **next** dc, YO and pull up a loop, YO and draw through 2 loops on hook; repeat from ★ 2 times **more**, YO and draw through all 4 loops on hook.
>
> **LONG HALF DOUBLE CROCHET**
>   **(abbreviated LHDC)**
> YO, insert hook around sts indicated, YO and pull up a loop even with loop on hook, YO and draw through all 3 loops on hook.

STRIP (Make 10)
CENTER

Ch 12 **loosely**, place marker in third ch from hook for st placement.

Row 1 (Right side): Dc in fourth ch from hook **(3 skipped chs count as first dc)**, ch 1, skip next 2 chs, (3 dc, ch 1, dc) in next ch, ch 3, skip next 3 chs, dc in last 2 chs: 8 dc.

Note: Loop a short piece of yarn around any stitch to mark Row 1 as **right** side and bottom edge.

Row 2: Ch 3 **(counts as first dc, now and throughout)**, turn; dc in next dc, ch 1, (3 dc, ch 1, dc) in next dc, ch 1, work Cluster, ch 1, dc in last 2 dc: 9 sts.

Rows 3-85: Ch 3, turn; dc in next dc, ch 1, skip next Cluster, (3 dc, ch 1, dc) in next dc, ch 1, work Cluster, ch 1, dc in last 2 dc; do **not** finish off.

BORDER
FIRST SIDE

Row 1: Ch 1, do **not** turn; sc in top of last dc made on Row 85; working across long edge of Center, work 2 LHDC around last 2 dc in end of same row, ★ inserting hook from **front** to **back**, dc around first ch on next row, work LHDC around last 2 dc on same row, inserting hook from **front** to **back**, dc around first ch on next row, work 2 LHDC around last 2 dc on same row; repeat from ★ across, sc in ch at base of last dc: 214 sts.

Row 2: Ch 1, turn; sc in Front Loop Only of each st across *(Fig. 2, page 143)*; finish off.

SECOND SIDE

Row 1: With **right** side facing and working across long edge of Center, join yarn with sc in marked ch *(see Joining With Sc, page 142)*; work 2 LHDC around first 2 dc on Row 1, ★ inserting hook from **front** to **back**, dc around first ch on same row, work LHDC around first 2 dc on next row, inserting hook from **front** to **back**, dc around first ch on same row, work 2 LHDC around first 2 dc on next row; repeat from ★ across, sc in top of first dc on Row 85: 214 sts.

Row 2: Ch 1, turn; sc in Front Loop Only of each st across; finish off.

ASSEMBLY

Whipstitch Strips together beginning in first sc and ending in last sc *(Fig. 9a, page 144)*.

TRIM
TOP

With **right** side facing, join yarn with sc in end of Row 2 on Second Side of Border at top right corner; working in end of rows and in sts across last row of Center, work 13 sc evenly spaced across to next joining, sc in joining, (work 14 sc evenly spaced across to next joining, sc in joining) 8 times, work 14 sc evenly spaced across to next corner; finish off: 149 sc.

Continued on page 79.

THIS ELEGANT BLANKET IS PERFECT FOR A BRIDAL SHOWER OR WEDDING GIFT. CREATED WITH AIRY STRIPS, IT CAPTURES THE CHARM OF LILIES OF THE VALLEY.

Rose of Sharon

Finished Size: 52" x 69"

MATERIALS
Worsted Weight Yarn:
   Lt Green - 18 ounces,
      (510 grams, 1,235 yards)
   Purple - 17³/₄ ounces, (500 grams, 1,220 yards)
   Green - 16 ounces, (450 grams, 1,095 yards)
Crochet hook, size H (5.00 mm) **or** size needed
   for gauge
Yarn needle

GAUGE: Each Square = 8"

Gauge Swatch: 3¹/₄" diameter
Work same as Square through Rnd 3.

STITCH GUIDE

TREBLE CROCHET (abbreviated tr)
YO twice, insert hook in st or sp indicated, YO
and pull up a loop (4 loops on hook), (YO and
draw through 2 loops on hook) 3 times.

2-DC CLUSTER (uses one st)
★ YO, insert hook in st indicated, YO and pull
up a loop, YO and draw through 2 loops on
hook; repeat from ★ once **more**, YO and draw
through all 3 loops on hook.

3-DC CLUSTER (uses one st)
★ YO, insert hook in st indicated, YO and pull
up a loop, YO and draw through 2 loops on
hook; repeat from ★ 2 times **more**, YO and
draw through all 4 loops on hook.

TR CLUSTER (uses one st)
★ YO twice, insert hook in st indicated, YO
and pull up a loop, (YO and draw through
2 loops on hook) twice; repeat from ★ 2 times
more, YO and draw through all 4 loops on
hook.

DC DECREASE
YO, † insert hook in **next** ch-1 sp, YO and pull
up a loop, YO and draw through 2 loops on
hook †, YO, skip next 3-dc Cluster, insert hook in
sp **before** next 3-dc Cluster **(Fig. 5, page 143)**,
YO and pull up a loop, YO and draw through
2 loops on hook, YO, skip next 3-dc Cluster,

repeat from † to † once, YO and draw through
all 4 loops on hook.

2-TR DECREASE
YO twice, insert hook in same sp as last leg of
3-tr decrease just made, YO and pull up a
loop, (YO and draw through 2 loops on hook)
twice, YO twice, skip next 2-dc Cluster, insert
hook in next ch-1 sp, YO and pull up a loop,
(YO and draw through 2 loops on hook) twice,
YO and draw through all 3 loops on hook.

3-TR DECREASE
YO twice, † insert hook in **next** ch-1 sp, YO
and pull up a loop, (YO and draw through
2 loops on hook) twice †, YO twice, skip next
3-dc Cluster, insert hook in sp **before** next
3-dc Cluster, YO and pull up a loop, (YO and
draw through 2 loops on hook) twice, YO
twice, skip next 3-dc Cluster, repeat from
† to † once, YO and draw through all 4 loops
on hook.

**BACK POST TREBLE CROCHET
   (abbreviated BPtr)**
YO twice, insert hook from **back** to **front** around
post of tr indicated **(Fig. 4, page 143)**, YO and
pull up a loop (4 loops on hook), (YO and draw
through 2 loops on hook) 3 times.

PICOT
Ch 4, slip st in back ridge of third ch from hook
(Fig. 1, page 143), ch 1.

SQUARE (Make 48)
With Purple, ch 6; join with slip st to form a ring.

Rnd 1 (Right side)**:** Ch 4, hdc in back ridge of
second ch from hook **(Fig. 1, page 143)**, ★ hdc in
ring, ch 2, hdc in back ridge of second ch from
hook; repeat from ★ 2 times **more**; join with slip st
to second ch of beginning ch-4: 4 petals.

Note: Loop a short piece of yarn around any stitch
to mark Rnd 1 as **right** side.

Rnd 2: Working in beginning ring **behind** Rnd 1
(Fig. 6, page 143), (dc, ch 3, work 2-dc Cluster in
back ridge of third ch from hook) twice in ring

Continued on page 80.

Nostalgic Pleasure

Finished Size: 49" x 66"

MATERIALS
Worsted Weight Yarn:
Black - 42 ounces, (1,190 grams, 2,375 yards)
Lt Green - 5 ounces, (140 grams, 285 yards)
Dk Green - 5 ounces, (140 grams, 285 yards)
Lt Plum - 3 ounces, (90 grams, 170 yards)
Dk Plum - 3 ounces, (90 grams, 170 yards)
Crochet hook, size I (5.50 mm) **or** size needed for gauge
Safety pin
Yarn needle

GAUGE: Each Square = 4¹/₄"

Gauge Swatch: 1³/₄" square
Work same as Square A through Rnd 1.

SQUARE A (Make 83)
Rnd 1 (Right side): With Black, ch 4, 2 dc in fourth ch from hook **(3 skipped chs count as first dc, now and throughout)**, ch 3, (3 dc in same ch, ch 3) 3 times; join with slip st to first dc, slip loop from hook onto safety pin to keep piece from unraveling while working next rnd: 12 dc and 4 ch-3 sps.

Note: Loop a short piece of yarn around any stitch to mark Rnd 1 as **right** side.

Keep dropped yarn and safety pin to **wrong** side, now and throughout.

Rnd 2: With **wrong** side facing, join Dk Plum with sc in any ch-3 sp **(see Joining With Sc, page 142)**; ch 3, sc in same sp, ch 1, skip next dc, sc in next dc, ch 1, ★ (sc, ch 3, sc) in next ch-3 sp, ch 1, skip next dc, sc in next dc, ch 1; repeat from ★ 2 times **more**; join with slip st to first sc, finish off: 12 sps.

Rnd 3: With **right** side facing and working **behind** Rnd 2, remove safety pin and place loop onto hook; ch 3 **(counts as first dc, now and throughout)**, sc in next sc, working **behind** next ch-1 **(Fig. 6, page 143)**, dc in skipped dc on

Rnd 1, sc in next sc on Rnd 2, ★ † working in **front** of next ch-3, (dc, ch 3, dc) in sp on Rnd 1 **before** next sc, sc in next sc on Rnd 2 †, (working **behind** next ch-1, dc in skipped dc on Rnd 1, sc in next sc on Rnd 2) twice; repeat from ★ 2 times **more**, then repeat from † to † once; join with slip st to first dc, slip loop from hook onto safety pin: 28 sts and 4 ch-3 sps.

Rnd 4: With **wrong** side facing, join Dk Green with sc in any corner ch-3 sp; ch 3, sc in same sp, ch 1, skip next dc, (sc in next sc, ch 1, skip next dc) 3 times, ★ (sc, ch 3, sc) in next ch-3 sp, ch 1, skip next dc, (sc in next sc, ch 1, skip next dc) 3 times; repeat from ★ 2 times **more**; join with slip st to first sc, finish off: 20 sps and 20 sc.

Rnd 5: With **right** side facing and working **behind** Rnd 4, remove safety pin and place loop onto hook; ch 3, sc in next sc, (working **behind** next ch-1, dc in skipped dc on Rnd 3, sc in next sc on Rnd 4) twice, ★ † working in **front** of next ch-3, (dc, ch 3, dc) in sp on Rnd 3 **before** next sc, sc in next sc on Rnd 4 †, (working **behind** next ch-1, dc in skipped dc on Rnd 3, sc in next sc on Rnd 4) 4 times; repeat from ★ 2 times **more**, then repeat from † to † once, working **behind** next ch-1, dc in skipped dc on Rnd 3, sc in last sc on Rnd 4; join with slip st to first dc, finish off: 44 sts and 4 ch-3 sps.

SQUARE B (Make 82)
Rnd 1 (Right side): With Black, ch 4, 2 dc in fourth ch from hook, ch 3, (3 dc in same ch, ch 3) 3 times; join with slip st to first dc, slip loop from hook onto safety pin: 12 dc and 4 ch-3 sps.

Note: Mark Rnd 1 as **right** side.

Rnd 2: With **wrong** side facing, join Lt Plum with sc in any ch-3 sp; ch 3, sc in same sp, ch 1, skip next dc, sc in next dc, ch 1, ★ (sc, ch 3, sc) in next ch-3 sp, ch 1, skip next dc, sc in next dc, ch 1; repeat from ★ 2 times **more**; join with slip st to first sc, finish off: 12 sps.

Continued on page 81.

THIS SUBTLY SHADED AFGHAN
RECALLS THE WILDFLOWER MEADOWS
SURROUNDING A COUNTRY CABIN.
ITS OLD-FASHIONED STYLE GIVES
IT ALL THE NOSTALGIA OF A
TREASURED HEIRLOOM.

Exquisite Flowers

Finished Size: 54" x 74"

MATERIALS
Worsted Weight Yarn:
    Blue - 39 ounces, (1,110 grams, 2,675 yards)
    Ecru - 5$\frac{1}{2}$ ounces, (160 grams, 375 yards)
Crochet hook, size G (4.00 mm) **or** size needed
    for gauge

GAUGE: Each Motif = 10" square

Gauge Swatch: 3$\frac{3}{4}$" diameter
Work same as First Motif through Rnd 2.

STITCH GUIDE

TREBLE CROCHET *(abbreviated tr)*
YO twice, insert hook in dc indicated, YO and
pull up a loop (4 loops on hook), (YO and draw
through 2 loops on hook) 3 times.

PICOT
Ch 3, slip st in top of last sc made *(Fig. 7, page 143)*.

BEGINNING CLUSTER (uses one st)
Ch 4, ★ YO 3 times, insert hook in **same** st, YO
and pull up a loop, (YO and draw through
2 loops on hook) 3 times; repeat from ★ once
more, YO and draw through all 3 loops on hook.

CLUSTER (uses one st)
★ YO 3 times, insert hook in sc indicated, YO
and pull up a loop, (YO and draw through
2 loops on hook) 3 times; repeat from ★
2 times **more**, YO and draw through all
4 loops on hook.

2-TR CLUSTER (uses one st)
★ YO twice, insert hook in st indicated, YO
and pull up a loop, (YO and draw through
2 loops on hook) twice; repeat from ★ once
more, YO and draw through all 3 loops on hook.

3-TR CLUSTER (uses one st)
★ YO twice, insert hook in st indicated, YO
and pull up a loop, (YO and draw through
2 loops on hook) twice; repeat from ★ 2 times
more, YO and draw through all 4 loops on hook.

FIRST MOTIF
With Ecru, ch 10; join with slip st to form a ring.

Rnd 1 (Right side)**:** Ch 1, (2 sc in ring, work
Picot) 8 times; join with slip st to first sc: 16 sc
and 8 Picots.

Note: Loop a short piece of yarn around any stitch
to mark Rnd 1 as **right** side.

Rnd 2: Work Beginning Cluster, ch 6, skip next sc
and next Picot, ★ work Cluster in next sc, ch 6,
skip next sc and next Picot; repeat from ★ around;
join with slip st to top of Beginning Cluster,
finish off: 8 Clusters and 8 ch-6 sps.

Rnd 3: With **right** side facing, join Blue with slip st
in any ch-6 sp; ch 3 **(counts as first dc, now and
throughout)**, 3 dc in same sp, dc in next Cluster,
(7 dc in next ch-6 sp, dc in next Cluster) around,
3 dc in same sp as first dc; join with slip st to first
dc: 64 dc.

Rnd 4: Ch 6 **(counts as first tr plus ch 2)**, skip
next dc, ★ tr in next dc, ch 2, skip next dc; repeat
from ★ around; join with slip st to first tr: 32 tr
and 32 ch-2 sps.

Rnd 5: Ch 3, 2 dc in next ch-2 sp, (dc in next tr,
2 dc in next ch-2 sp) around; join with slip st to
first dc: 96 dc.

Rnd 6: Ch 1, sc in same st, ★ ch 5, skip next 2 dc,
sc in next dc; repeat from ★ around to last 2 dc,
ch 2, skip last 2 dc, dc in first sc to form last
ch-5 sp: 32 ch-5 sps.

Rnd 7: Ch 1, sc in last ch-5 sp made, ch 5, work
3-tr Cluster in center ch of next ch-5, (ch 7, work
3-tr Cluster in center ch of next ch-5) twice,
★ ch 5, (sc in next ch-5 sp, ch 5) 5 times, work
3-tr Cluster in center ch of next ch-5, (ch 7, work
3-tr Cluster in center ch of next ch-5) twice; repeat
from ★ 2 times **more**, (ch 5, sc in next ch-5 sp) 4
times, ch 2, dc in first sc to form last ch-5 sp; do
not finish off: 12 3-tr Clusters and 32 sps.

Continued on page 74.

Rnd 8: Ch 1, sc in last ch-5 sp made, ch 5, sc in next ch-5 sp, ch 6, (slip st, ch 4, work 2-tr Cluster) in center ch of next ch-7, ch 7, (work 2-tr Cluster, ch 4, slip st) in center ch of next ch-7, ch 6, ★ sc in next ch-5 sp, (ch 5, sc in next ch-5 sp) 5 times, ch 6, (slip st, ch 4, work 2-tr Cluster) in center ch of next ch-7, ch 7, (work 2-tr Cluster, ch 4, slip st) in center ch of next ch-7, ch 6; repeat from ★ 2 times **more**, (sc in next ch-5 sp, ch 5) 4 times; join with slip st to first sc, finish off: 8 2-tr Clusters and 24 sc.

ADDITIONAL 34 MOTIFS

The method used to connect the Motifs is a no-sew joining also known as "join-as-you-go". After the First Motif is made, each remaining Motif is worked through Rnd 7, then crocheted together as Rnd 8 is worked.

Work same as First Motif through Rnd 7; do **not** finish off: 12 3-tr Cluster and 32 sps.

Rnd 8 (Joining rnd): Work One or Two Side Joining **(Fig. 10, page 144)**, arranging Motifs into 5 vertical strips of 7 Motifs each.

When joining to a Motif that has been previously joined, work slip st in same ch.

ONE SIDE JOINING

Rnd 8 (Joining rnd): Ch 1, sc in last ch-5 sp made, ch 5, sc in next ch-5 sp, ch 6, (slip st, ch 4, work 2-tr Cluster) in center ch of next ch-7, ★ ch 7, (work 2-tr Cluster, ch 4, slip st) in center ch of next ch-7, ch 6, sc in next ch-5 sp, (ch 5, sc in next ch-5 sp) 5 times, ch 6, (slip st, ch 4, work 2-tr Cluster) in center ch of next ch-7; repeat from ★ once **more**, ch 3, holding Motifs with **wrong** sides together, slip st in center ch of corner ch-7 on **previous Motif**, ch 3, (work 2-tr Cluster, ch 4, slip st) in center ch of next ch-7 on **new Motif**, ch 3, slip st in next ch-6 sp on **previous Motif**, (ch 2, sc in next ch-5 sp on **new Motif**, ch 2, slip st in next sp on **previous Motif**) 6 times, ch 3, (slip st, ch 4, work 2-tr Cluster) in center ch of next ch-7 on **new Motif**, ch 3, slip st in center ch of corner ch-7 on **previous Motif**, ch 3, (work 2-tr Cluster, ch 4, slip st) in center ch of next ch-7 on **new Motif**, ch 6, (sc in next ch-5 sp, ch 5) 4 times; join with slip st to first sc, finish off.

TWO SIDE JOINING

Rnd 8 (Joining rnd): Ch 1, sc in last ch-5 sp made, ch 5, sc in next ch-5 sp, ch 6, (slip st, ch 4, work 2-tr Cluster) in center ch of next ch-7, ch 7, (work 2-tr Cluster, ch 4, slip st) in center ch of next ch-7, ch 6, sc in next ch-5 sp, (ch 5, sc in next ch-5 sp) 5 times, ch 6, (slip st, ch 4, work 2-tr Cluster) in center ch of next ch-7, ch 3, holding Motifs with **wrong** sides together, slip st in center ch of corner ch-7 on **previous Motif**, ch 3, (work 2-tr Cluster, ch 4, slip st) in center ch of next ch-7 on **new Motif**, ★ ch 3, slip st in corresponding ch-6 sp on **previous Motif**, (ch 2, sc in next ch-5 sp on **new Motif**, ch 2, slip st in next sp on **previous Motif**) 6 times, ch 3, (slip st, ch 4, work 2-tr Cluster) in center ch of next ch-7 on **new Motif**, ch 3, slip st in center ch of corner ch-7 on **previous Motif**, ch 3, (work 2-tr Cluster, ch 4, slip st) in center ch of next ch-7 on **new Motif**; repeat from ★ once **more**, ch 6, (sc in next ch-5 sp, ch 5) 4 times; join with slip st to first sc, finish off.

EDGING

Rnd 1: With **right** side facing, join Blue with sc in center ch of any corner ch-7 **(see Joining With Sc, page 142)**; ch 6, ★ † sc in top of next 2-tr Cluster, ch 6, skip next slip st, (sc in next sp, ch 6) 7 times, sc in next slip st, ch 6, sc in top of next 2-tr Cluster, ch 6, [skip next joining, sc in top of next 2-tr Cluster, ch 6, sc in next slip st, ch 6, (sc in next sp, ch 6) 7 times, sc in next slip st, ch 6, sc in top of next 2-tr Cluster, ch 6] across to next corner ch-7 †, (sc, ch 6) twice in center ch of corner ch-7; repeat from ★ 2 times **more**, then repeat from † to † once, sc in same ch as first sc, ch 3, dc in first sc to form last ch-6 sp: 268 ch-6 sps.

Rnds 2 and 3: Ch 1, sc in last ch-6 sp made, ch 6, (sc in next ch-6 sp, ch 6) across to next corner ch-6 sp, ★ (sc, ch 6) twice in corner ch-6 sp, (sc in next ch-6 sp, ch 6) across to next corner ch-6 sp; repeat from ★ 2 times **more**, sc in same sp as first sc, ch 3, dc in first sc to form last ch-6 sp: 276 ch-6 sps.

Rnd 4: Ch 3, 4 dc in last ch-6 sp made, sc in next ch-6 sp, ★ (5 dc in next ch-6 sp, sc in next ch-6 sp) across to next corner ch-6 sp, 7 dc in corner ch-6 sp, sc in next ch-6 sp; repeat from ★ 2 times **more**, (5 dc in next ch-6 sp, sc in next ch-6 sp) across, 2 dc in same sp as first dc; join with slip st to first dc: 836 sts.

Rnd 5: Ch 2, sc in second ch from hook, skip next dc, ★ slip st in next dc, ch 2, sc in second ch from hook, skip next st; repeat from ★ around; join with slip st to same st as joining, finish off.

Design by Shobha Govindan.

LAVENDER LACE
Continued from page 52.

Rnd 2: With **right** side facing, join Ecru with slip st in first ch-5 sp; ch 6, (dc, ch 3, dc) in same sp, ★ decrease working second leg in next ch-5 sp, dc in same sp, (ch 3, dc in same sp) twice; repeat from ★ around, decrease working second leg in same sp as beginning ch-6; join with slip st to third ch of beginning ch-6, finish off: 184 ch-3 sps.

REMAINING 8 STRIPS
The method used to connect the Strips is a no-sew joining also known as "join-as-you-go". After the First Strip is made, each remaining Strip is worked through Rnd 1, then crocheted together as Rnd 2 is worked *(Fig. 10, page 144)*.

Work same as First Strip through Rnd 1 of Border: 92 ch-5 sps.

Rnd 2 (Joining rnd): With **right** side facing, join Ecru with slip st in last ch-5 sp; ch 6, dc in same sp, decrease working second leg in next ch-5 sp, ★ dc in same sp, (ch 3, dc in same sp) twice, decrease working second leg in next ch-5 sp; repeat from ★ 47 times **more**, (dc, ch 3, dc) in same sp, ch 1, holding Strips with **wrong** sides together, slip st in corresponding ch-3 sp on **previous Strip**, ch 1, dc in same sp on **new Strip**, † decrease working second leg in next ch-5 sp, dc in same sp, (ch 1, slip st in next ch-3 sp on **previous Strip**, ch 1, dc in same sp on **new Strip**) twice †; repeat from † to † across, decrease working second leg in same ch-5 sp as beginning ch-6, dc in same sp, ch 1, slip st in next ch-3 sp on **previous Strip**, ch 1; join with slip st to third ch of beginning ch-6 on **new Strip**, finish off.

Design by Tammy Kreimeyer.

EYE-CATCHING POSIES
Continued from page 54.

ch 1, † skip next dc on **new Square**, sc in next dc, ch 1, drop loop from hook, insert hook from **back** to **front** in next ch-2 sp on **previous Square**, hook dropped loop and pull through, ch 1 †; repeat from † to † 5 times **more**, skip next dc on **new Square**, sc in next corner ch-3 sp, ch 1, drop loop from hook, insert hook from **back** to **front** in next corner ch-3 sp on **previous Square**, hook dropped loop and pull through, ch 2, sc in same sp on **new Square**, ch 2, skip next dc, (sc in next dc, ch 2, skip next st) 3 times; join with slip st to first sc, finish off.

TWO SIDE JOINING
Rnd 5 (Joining rnd): Slip st in next dc, ch 1, sc in same st, ch 2, skip next dc, (sc in next dc, ch 2, skip next dc) twice, (sc, ch 3, sc) in next corner ch-3 sp, ch 2, skip next dc, (sc in next dc, ch 2, skip next dc) 6 times, sc in next corner ch-3 sp, ch 1, holding Squares with **wrong** sides together, drop loop from hook, insert hook from **back** to **front** in corresponding corner ch-3 sp on **previous Square**, hook dropped loop and pull through, ch 2, sc in same sp on **new Square**, † ch 1, drop loop from hook, insert hook from **back** to **front** in next ch-2 sp on **previous Square**, hook dropped loop and pull through, ch 1, ★ skip next dc on **new Square**, sc in next dc, ch 1, drop loop from hook, insert hook from **back** to **front** in next ch-2 sp on **previous Square**, hook dropped loop and pull through, ch 1; repeat from ★ 5 times **more**, skip next dc on **new Square**, sc in next corner ch-3 sp, ch 1, drop loop from hook, insert hook from **back** to **front** in next corner sp on **previous Square**, hook dropped loop and pull through, ch 2, sc in same sp on **new Square** †; repeat from † to † once **more**, ch 2, skip next dc, (sc in next dc, ch 2, skip next st) 3 times; join with slip st to first sc, finish off.

Design by Maggie Weldon.

PANSY DELIGHT

Continued from page 56.

Rnd 2: With **right** side facing, join Ecru with slip st in first corner ch-3 sp; ch 3, 2 dc in same sp, ch 1, (3 dc, ch 3, 3 dc) in next corner ch-3 sp, ch 1, (3 dc in next ch-1 sp, ch 1) 7 times, [(3 dc, ch 3, 3 dc) in next corner ch-3 sp, ch 1] twice, (3 dc in next ch-1 sp, ch 1) 7 times, 3 dc in same sp as first dc, dc in first dc to form last ch-3 sp: 22 sps.

Rnd 3: Ch 3, (2 dc, ch 3, 3 dc) in last ch-3 sp made, † ch 1, 3 dc in next ch-1 sp, ch 1, (3 dc, ch 3, 3 dc) in next corner ch-3 sp, ch 1, (3 dc in next ch-1 sp, ch 1) 8 times †, (3 dc, ch 3, 3 dc) in next corner ch-3 sp, repeat from † to † once; join with slip st to first dc, finish off: 26 sps.

ASSEMBLY

With Ecru, using Placement Diagram as a guide, and working through **inside** loops only, whipstitch Squares and Rectangles together forming 12 vertical strips of 5 Squares and 4 rectangles each **(Fig. 9b, page 144)**, beginning in center ch of first corner ch-3 and ending in center ch of next corner ch-3; then whipstitch strips together in same manner.

EDGING

With **right** side facing and working across short edge of Afghan, join Green with slip st in first corner ch-3 sp; ch 3, (2 dc, ch 3, 3 dc) in same sp, † ch 1, (3 dc in next ch-1 sp, ch 1) twice, [dc in next sp, decrease, dc in same sp, ch 1, (3 dc in next ch-1 sp, ch 1) twice] across to next corner ch-3 sp, (3 dc, ch 3, 3 dc) in corner ch-3 sp, ch 1, (3 dc in next ch-1 sp, ch 1) twice, ★ dc in next sp, decrease, dc in same sp, ch 1, (3 dc in next ch-1 sp, ch 1) 9 times, dc in next sp, decrease, dc in same sp, ch 1, (3 dc in next ch-1 sp, ch 1) twice; repeat from ★ across to next corner ch-3 sp †, (3 dc, ch 3, 3 dc) in corner ch-3 sp, repeat from † to † once; join with slip st to first dc, finish off.

Design by Maggie Weldon.

PLACEMENT DIAGRAM

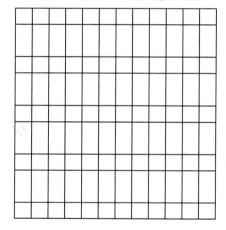

ROSY DREAM Continued from page 58.

Rnd 5: With **right** side facing, join Green with slip st in any corner ch-5 sp; ch 3, (dc, ch 3, 2 dc) in same sp, 3 dc in each of next 5 ch-5 sps, ★ (2 dc, ch 3, 2 dc) in next corner ch-5 sp, 3 dc in each of next 5 ch-5 sps; repeat from ★ 2 times **more**; join with slip st to first dc, finish off: 76 dc and 4 ch-3 sps.

Rnd 6: With **right** side facing, join Ecru with sc in first dc to right of any corner ch-3 sp **(see Joining With Sc, page 142)**; ★ † working in **front** of Rnd 5 **(Fig. 6, page 143)** and **between** 2-dc groups, work LDC in ch-5 sp on Rnd 4, 3 sc in corner ch-3 sp on Rnd 5, working in **front** of Rnd 5, work LDC in same sp as last LDC made, sc in next dc on Rnd 5, skip next dc, YO, insert hook in same corner sp on Rnd 4 **after** last 2-dc group, YO and pull up a loop even with loop on hook, YO and draw through 2 loops on hook, YO, insert hook in next ch-5 sp on Rnd 4 **before** next 3-dc group, YO and pull up a loop even with loop on hook, YO and draw through 2 loops on hook, YO and draw through all 3 loops on hook, (sc in next 3 dc on Rnd 5, decrease) 5 times, skip next dc on Rnd 5 †, sc in next dc; repeat from ★ 2 times **more**, then repeat from † to † once; join with slip st to first sc, finish off: 112 sts.

ASSEMBLY

With Ecru, whipstitch Squares together forming 6 vertical strips of 8 Squares each **(Fig. 9a, page 144)**, beginning in center sc of first corner 3-sc group and ending in center sc of next corner 3-sc group; then whipstitch strips together in same manner.

EDGING

Rnd 1: With **right** side facing, join Ecru with sc in center sc of any corner 3-sc group; ch 5, sc in same st, ★ † ch 5, skip next 3 sts, (sc in next st, ch 5, skip next 3 sts) 6 times, [sc in next joining, ch 5, skip next 3 sts, (sc in next st, ch 5, skip next 3 sts) 6 times] across to center sc of next corner 3-sc group †, (sc, ch 5, sc) in center sc; repeat from ★ 2 times **more**, then repeat from † to † once; join with slip st to first sc, finish off: 200 ch-5 sps.

Rnd 2: With **right** side facing, join Rose with slip st in any corner ch-5 sp; ch 3, (dc, ch 3, 2 dc) in same sp, ★ 3 dc in next ch-5 sp and in each ch-5 sp across to next corner ch-5 sp, (2 dc, ch 3, 2 dc) in corner ch-5 sp; repeat from ★ 2 times **more**, 3 dc in next ch-5 sp and in each ch-5 sp across; join with slip st to first dc, finish off: 604 dc and 4 ch-3 sps.

Rnd 3: With **right** side facing, join Ecru with sc in any corner ch-3 sp; ★ † work Cluster, sc in same sp, working in **front** of Rnd 2, work LDC in ch-5 sp one rnd **below** same corner ch-3 **between** 2-dc groups, work Cluster, skip next 2 dc, YO, working in **front** of Rnd 2, insert hook in same corner sp on Rnd 1 **after** last 2-dc group, YO and pull up a loop, YO and draw through 2 loops on hook, YO, insert hook in next ch-5 sp on Rnd 1 **before** next 3-dc group, YO and pull up a loop, YO and draw through 2 loops on hook, YO and draw through all 3 loops on hook, (sc in next dc on Rnd 2, work Cluster, skip next dc, sc in next dc, decrease) across to next corner 2-dc group, work Cluster, skip next 2 dc on Rnd 2 †, working in **front** of Rnd 2, work LDC in ch-5 sp one rnd **below** next corner ch-3 **between** 2-dc groups, sc in corner ch-3 sp on Rnd 2; repeat from ★ 2 times **more**, then repeat from † to † once, working in **front** of Rnd 2, work LDC in same sp one rnd **below** first corner ch-3 as first LDC **between** 2 dc-groups; join with slip st to first sc, finish off.

Design by Tammy Kreimeyer.

SEED-PACKET PORTRAITS
Continued from page 60.

ONE SIDE JOINING
Rnd 8 (Joining rnd): Slip st in both loops of next sc, ch 1, (sc, ch 3) twice in same st, skip next sc, (sc in next sc, ch 3, skip next sc) across to center sc of next corner 3-sc group, (sc, ch 3) twice in center sc, skip next sc, (sc in next sc, ch 3, skip next sc) across to center sc of next corner 3-sc group, sc in center sc, ch 1; holding Squares with **wrong** sides together, sc in corresponding corner ch-3 sp on **previous Square**, ch 1, sc in same st on **new Square**, ch 1, sc in next ch-3 sp on **previous Square**, ch 1, skip next sc on **new Square**, ★ sc in next sc, ch 1, sc in next ch-3 sp on **previous Square**, ch 1, skip next sc on **new Square**; repeat from ★ across to center sc of next corner 3-sc group, sc in center sc, ch 1, sc in corner ch-3 sp on **previous Square**, ch 1, sc in same st on **new Square**, ch 3, skip next sc, (sc in next sc, ch 3, skip next sc) across; join with slip st to first sc, finish off.

TWO SIDE JOINING
Rnd 8 (Joining rnd): Slip st in both loops of next sc, ch 1, (sc, ch 3) twice in same st, skip next sc, (sc in next sc, ch 3, skip next sc) across to center sc of next corner 3-sc group, sc in center sc, ch 1; holding Squares with **wrong** sides together, sc in corresponding corner ch-3 sp on **previous Square**, ch 1, sc in same st on **new Square**, † ch 1, sc in next ch-3 sp on **previous Square**, ch 1, skip next sc on **new Square**, ★ sc in next sc, ch 1, sc in next ch-3 sp on **previous Square**, ch 1, skip next sc on **new Square**; repeat from ★ across to center sc of next corner 3-sc group, sc in center sc, ch 1, sc in corner ch-3 sp on **previous Square**, ch 1, sc in same st on **new Square** †; repeat from † to † once, ch 3, skip next sc, (sc in next sc, ch 3, skip next sc) across; join with slip st to first sc, finish off.

EDGING
Rnd 1: With **right** side facing, join Off-White with dc in any corner ch-3 sp; 2 dc in same sp and in each sp across to next corner ch-3 sp, ★ 3 dc in corner ch-3 sp, 2 dc in each sp across to next corner ch-3 sp; repeat from ★ 2 times **more**; join with slip st to first dc, finish off: 836 dc.

Rnd 2: With **right** side facing and working in Back Loops Only, join Green with sc in any dc; sc in each dc around working 3 sc in center dc of each corner 3-dc group; join with slip st to first sc, finish off.

Design by Sue Galucki.

TEATIME TULIPS
Continued from page 62.

Rnd 4: With **right** side facing and working **around** ch-sps on Rnd 3 and in sps and sts on Rnd 2 **(Fig. 6, page 143)**, join Ecru with hdc in first ch-3 sp **(see Joining With Hdc, page 142)**; (hdc, 2 dc) in same sp, † 3 tr in next Cluster, (2 dc, 2 hdc) in next ch-3 sp, ch 3, ★ 2 hdc in next ch-3 sp, work LSC in sp **between** Legs of next Split Cluster, 2 hdc in next ch-3 sp, ch 3; repeat from ★ 40 times **more** †, (2 hdc, 2 dc) in next ch-3 sp, repeat from † to † once; join with slip st to first hdc, finish off: 84 ch-3 sps.

REMAINING 11 STRIPS
The method used to connect the Strips is a no-sew joining also known as "join-as-you-go". After the First Strip is made, each remaining Strip is worked through Rnd 3, then crocheted together as Rnd 4 is worked **(Fig. 10, page 144)**.

Work same as First Strip through Rnd 3: 84 FP Clusters.

Rnd 4 (Joining rnd): With **right** side facing and working **around** ch-sps on Rnd 3 and in sps and sts on Rnd 2, join Ecru with hdc in first ch-3 sp; (hdc, 2 dc) in same sp, 3 tr in next Cluster, (2 dc, 2 hdc) in next ch-3 sp, ch 3, ★ 2 hdc in next ch-3 sp, work LSC in sp **between** Legs of next Split Cluster, 2 hdc in next ch-3 sp, ch 3; repeat from ★ 40 times **more**, (2 hdc, 2 dc) in next ch-3 sp, 3 tr in next Cluster, (2 dc, 2 hdc) in next ch-3 sp, ch 3, 2 hdc in next ch-3 sp, work LSC in sp **between** Legs of next Split Cluster, 2 hdc in next ch-3 sp, holding Strips with **wrong** sides together, † ch 1, slip st in corresponding ch-3 sp on **previous Strip**, ch 1, 2 hdc in next ch-3 sp on **new Strip**, work LSC in sp **between** Legs of next Split Cluster, 2 hdc in next ch-3 sp †; repeat from † to † across, ch 3; join with slip st to first hdc, finish off.

Design by Tammy Kreimeyer.

CHEERY GARDEN
Continued from page 64.

Rnd 3: With **right** side facing, join Green with sc in second sc of any corner 2-sc group; 2 sc in same st, ch 1, (skip next sc, sc in next sc, ch 1) across to next corner 2-sc group, skip next sc, ★ 3 sc in next sc, ch 1, (skip next sc, sc in next sc, ch 1) across to next corner 2-sc group, skip next sc; repeat from ★ 2 times **more**; join with slip st to first sc, finish off: 40 sc and 32 ch-1 sps.

Rnd 4: With **right** side facing, join White with sc in center sc of any corner 3-sc group; sc in same st, ch 1, (sc in next ch-1 sp, ch 1) across to next corner 3-sc group, skip next sc, ★ 3 sc in next sc, ch 1, (sc in next ch-1 sp, ch 1) across to next corner 3-sc group, skip next sc; repeat from ★ 2 times **more**, sc in same st as first sc; join with slip st to first sc: 44 sc and 36 ch-1 sps.

Rnd 5: Ch 1, 3 sc in same st, ch 1, (sc in next ch-1 sp, ch 1) across to next corner 3-sc group, skip next sc, ★ 3 sc in next sc, ch 1, (sc in next ch-1 sp, ch 1) across to next corner 3-sc group, skip next sc; repeat from ★ 2 times **more**; join with slip st to first sc, finish off: 48 sc and 40 ch-1 sps.

Rnd 6: With **right** side facing, join Green with sc in center sc of any corner 3-sc group; 2 sc in same st, ch 1, (sc in next ch-1 sp, ch 1) across to next corner 3-sc group, skip next sc, ★ 3 sc in next sc, ch 1, (sc in next ch-1 sp, ch 1) across to next corner 3-sc group, skip next sc; repeat from ★ 2 times **more**; join with slip st to first sc, finish off: 52 sc and 44 ch-1 sps.

Rnds 7 and 8: Repeat Rnds 4 and 5: 60 sc and 52 ch-1 sps.

ASSEMBLY

With White, randomly placing Squares as desired, and working through **both** loops, whipstitch Squares together forming 6 vertical strips of 8 Squares each **(Fig. 9a, page 144)**, beginning in center sc of first corner 3-sc group and ending in center sc of next corner 3-sc group; then whipstitch strips together in same manner.

EDGING

Rnd 1: With **right** side facing, join Green with sc in center sc of any corner 3-sc group; sc in same st, ch 1, (sc in next ch-1 sp, ch 1) 13 times, † sc in same st as joining on same Square, ch 1, sc in same st as joining on next Square, ch 1, (sc in next ch-1 sp, ch 1) 13 times †, repeat from † to † across to next corner 3-sc group, skip next sc, ★ 3 sc in next sc, ch 1, (sc in next ch-1 sp, ch 1) 13 times, repeat from † to † across to next corner 3-sc group, skip next sc; repeat from ★ 2 times **more**, sc in same st as first sc; join with slip st to first sc: 424 sc and 416 ch-1 sps.

Rnds 2-4: Ch 1, 2 sc in same st, ch 1, (sc in next ch-1 sp, ch 1) across to next corner 3-sc group, skip next sc, ★ 3 sc in next sc, ch 1, (sc in next ch-1 sp, ch 1) across to next corner 3-sc group, skip next sc; repeat from ★ 2 times **more**, sc in same st as first sc; join with slip st to first sc.

Finish off.

Design by Judith Gayler.

ELEGANT CHARM
Continued from page 66.

BOTTOM

With **right** side facing, join yarn with sc in end of Row 2 on First Side of Border at lower left corner; working in end of rows and in free loops of beginning ch **(Fig. 3b, page 143)**, work 13 sc evenly spaced across to next joining, sc in joining, (work 14 sc evenly spaced across to next joining, sc in joining) 8 times, work 14 sc evenly spaced across to next corner; do **not** finish off: 149 sc.

EDGING

Rnd 1: Ch 1, 2 sc in top of last sc made **(Fig. 7, page 143)**, sc in each sc across to first sc on Trim Top, 3 sc in first sc, sc in each sc across to last sc on Trim Top, 3 sc in last sc, sc in each sc across to first sc on Trim Bottom, 3 sc in first sc, sc in each sc across and in same st as first sc; join with slip st to first sc: 734 sc.

Rnd 2: Ch 1, sc in same st, ch 3, slip st in top of sc just made and in next sc, ★ sc in next sc, ch 3, slip st in top of sc just made and in next sc; repeat from ★ around; join with slip st to first sc, finish off.

Design by Tammy Kreimeyer.

79

ROSE OF SHARON

Continued from page 68.

before next hdc *(Fig. 5, page 143)*, ★ skip next hdc, (dc, work 2-dc Cluster in back ridge of third ch from hook) twice in ring **before** next hdc; repeat from ★ 2 times **more**; join with slip st to first dc: 8 petals.

Rnd 3: Working in beginning ring **behind** Rnds 1 and 2, skip first dc, ★ tr in ring **before** next dc, ch 4, work tr Cluster in back ridge of fourth ch from hook, skip next dc, tr in ring **before** next hdc, ch 4, work tr Cluster in back ridge of fourth ch from hook, skip next 2 sts; repeat from ★ around; join with slip st to first tr, finish off.

Rnd 4: With **right** side facing, join Lt Green with slip st from **back** to **front** around post of any tr *(Fig. 4, page 143)*; ch 6 **(counts as first BPtr plus ch 2)**, tr in back ridge of sixth ch from hook, ch 2, ★ work BPtr around next tr, ch 2, tr in back 2 legs of BPtr just made *(Fig. 1)*, ch 2; repeat from ★ around; join with slip st to first BPtr, do **not** finish off: 16 sts and 16 ch-2 sps.

Fig. 1

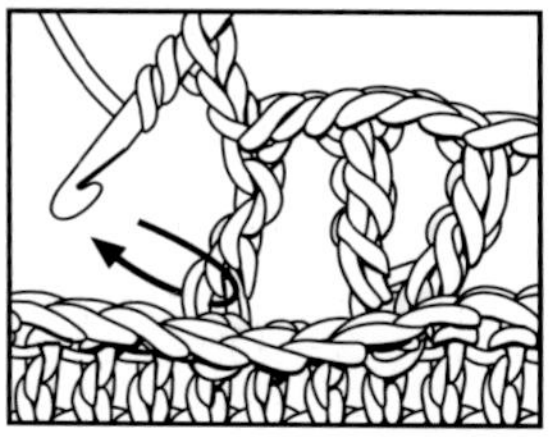

Rnd 5: Ch 2, (YO, insert hook in **same** st, YO and pull up a loop, YO and draw through 2 loops on hook) twice, YO and draw through all 3 loops on hook **(Beginning Cluster made)**, ch 4, work 2-dc Cluster in back ridge of third ch from hook, ch 1, work 3-dc Cluster in same st as Beginning Cluster, skip next ch-2 sp, ★ in next st work (3-dc Cluster, ch 4, 2-dc Cluster in back ridge of third ch from hook, ch 1, 3-dc Cluster), skip next ch-2 sp; repeat from ★ around; join with slip st to top of Beginning Cluster, finish off: 48 Clusters.

Rnd 6: With **right** side facing, join Green with slip st in ch-1 sp to **right** of any 2-dc Cluster; ch 3, skip next 2-dc Cluster, tr in next ch-1 sp, ch 3, ★ † YO twice, insert hook in **same** sp as last st made, YO and pull up a loop, (YO and draw through 2 loops on hook) twice, YO twice, skip next 3-dc Cluster, insert hook in sp **before** next 3-dc Cluster, YO and pull up a loop, (YO and draw through 2 loops on hook) twice, YO twice,

skip next 3-dc Cluster, insert hook in next ch-1 sp, YO and pull up a loop, (YO and draw through 2 loops on hook) twice, YO and draw through all 4 loops on hook, ch 3, skip next 2-dc Cluster, (dc decrease, ch 3, skip next 2-dc Cluster) twice †, work 3-tr decrease, ch 3, work 2-tr decrease, ch 3; repeat from ★ 2 times **more**, then repeat from † to † once, YO twice, insert hook in next ch-1 sp, YO and pull up a loop, (YO and draw through 2 loops on hook) twice, YO twice, skip next 3-dc Cluster, insert hook in sp **before** next 3-dc Cluster, YO and pull up a loop, (YO and draw through 2 loops on hook) twice, YO twice, insert hook in same sp as beginning ch-3, YO and pull up a loop, (YO and draw through 2 loops on hook) twice, YO and draw through all 4 loops on hook, ch 3; join with slip st to first tr, do **not** finish off: 20 sts and 20 ch-3 sps.

Rnd 7: Ch 3 **(counts as first dc)**, 4 dc in same st, 3 hdc in next ch-3 sp, sc in next st, (3 sc in next ch-3 sp, sc in next st) 3 times, 3 hdc in next ch-3 sp, ★ 5 dc in next st, 3 hdc in next ch-3 sp, sc in next st, (3 sc in next ch-3 sp, sc in next st) 3 times, 3 hdc in next ch-3 sp; repeat from ★ 2 times **more**; join with slip st to first dc, finish off: 96 sts.

Rnd 8: With **right** side facing and working in Back Loops Only *(Fig. 2, page 143)*, join Purple with sc in center dc of any corner 5-dc group **(see Joining With Sc, page 142)**; 2 sc in same st, ★ sc in each st across to center dc of next corner 5-dc group, 3 sc in center dc; repeat from ★ 2 times **more**, sc in each st across; join with slip st to first sc, finish off: 104 sc.

ASSEMBLY

With Purple and working through **inside** loops, whipstitch Squares together forming 6 vertical strips of 8 Squares each *(Fig. 9b, page 144)*, beginning in center sc of first corner 3-sc group and ending in center sc of next corner 3-sc group; then whipstitch strips together in same manner.

EDGING

Rnd 1: With **right** side facing and working in Back Loops Only, join Purple with sc in center sc of top right corner 3-sc group; sc in same st, † sc in next 25 sc, (sc in same st as joining on same Square and on next Square, sc in next 25 sc) twice, sc in next joining, sc in next 25 sc, (sc in same st as joining on same Square and on next Square, sc in next 25 sc) twice, 3 sc in center sc of next corner

3-sc group, sc in next 25 sc, (sc in same st as joining on same Square and on next Square, sc in next 25 sc) 3 times, sc in next joining, sc in next 25 sc, (sc in same st as joining on same Square and on next Square, sc in next 25 sc) 3 times †, 3 sc in center sc of next corner 3-sc group, repeat from † to † once, sc in same st as first sc; join with slip st to **both** loops of first sc: 756 sc.

Rnd 2: Ch 1, working in both loops, (sc in same st, work Picot) twice, ★ skip next 2 sc, (sc in next sc, work Picot, skip next 2 sc) across to center sc of next corner 3-sc group, (sc, work Picot) twice in center sc; repeat from ★ 2 times **more**, skip next 2 sc, (sc in next sc, work Picot, skip next 2 sc) across; join with slip st to first sc, finish off.

Design by Tammy Kreimeyer.

NOSTALGIC PLEASURE
Continued from page 70.

Rnd 3: With **right** side facing and working **behind** Rnd 2, remove safety pin and place loop onto hook; ch 3, sc in next sc, working **behind** next ch-1, dc in skipped dc on Rnd 1, sc in next sc on Rnd 2, ★ † working in **front** of next ch-3, (dc, ch 3, dc) in sp on Rnd 1 **before** next sc, sc in next sc on Rnd 2 †, (working **behind** next ch-1, dc in skipped dc on Rnd 1, sc in next sc on Rnd 2) twice; repeat from ★ 2 times **more**, then repeat from † to † once; join with slip st to first dc, slip loop from hook onto safety pin: 28 sts and 4 ch-3 sps.

Rnd 4: With **wrong** side facing, join Lt Green with sc in any corner ch-3 sp; ch 3, sc in same sp, ch 1, skip next dc, (sc in next sc, ch 1, skip next dc) 3 times, ★ (sc, ch 3, sc) in next ch-3 sp, ch 1, skip next dc, (sc in next sc, ch 1, skip next dc) 3 times; repeat from ★ 2 times **more**; join with slip st to first sc, finish off: 20 sps and 20 sc.

Rnd 5: With **right** side facing and working **behind** Rnd 4, remove safety pin and place loop onto hook; ch 3, sc in next sc, (working **behind** next ch-1, dc in skipped dc on Rnd 3, sc in next sc on Rnd 4) twice, ★ † working in **front** of next ch-3, (dc, ch 3, dc) in sp on Rnd 3 **before** next sc, sc in next sc on Rnd 4 †, (working **behind** next ch-1, dc in skipped dc on Rnd 3, sc in next sc on Rnd 4) 4 times; repeat from ★ 2 times **more**, then repeat from † to † once, working **behind** next ch-1, dc in skipped dc on Rnd 3, sc in last sc on Rnd 4; join with slip st to first dc, finish off: 44 sts and 4 ch-3 sps.

ASSEMBLY
With Black and using Placement Diagram as a guide, whipstitch Squares together forming 11 vertical strips of 15 Squares each **(Fig. 9a, page 144)**, beginning in center ch of first corner ch-3 and ending in center ch of next corner ch-3; then whipstitch strips together in same manner.

PLACEMENT DIAGRAM

A	B	A	B	A	B	A	B	A	B	A
B	A	B	A	B	A	B	A	B	A	B
A	B	A	B	A	B	A	B	A	B	A
B	A	B	A	B	A	B	A	B	A	B
A	B	A	B	A	B	A	B	A	B	A
B	A	B	A	B	A	B	A	B	A	B
A	B	A	B	A	B	A	B	A	B	A
B	A	B	A	B	A	B	A	B	A	B
A	B	A	B	A	B	A	B	A	B	A
B	A	B	A	B	A	B	A	B	A	B
A	B	A	B	A	B	A	B	A	B	A
B	A	B	A	B	A	B	A	B	A	B
A	B	A	B	A	B	A	B	A	B	A
B	A	B	A	B	A	B	A	B	A	B
A	B	A	B	A	B	A	B	A	B	A

EDGING
Rnd 1: With **wrong** side facing, join Black with sc in any corner ch-3 sp; ch 2, sc in same sp, ★ † ch 1, (skip next dc, sc in next sc, ch 1) 5 times, skip next dc, [sc in next sp, ch 1, skip next joining, sc in next sp, ch 1, skip next dc, (sc in next sc, ch 1, skip next dc) 5 times] across to next corner ch-3 sp †, (sc, ch 2, sc) in corner ch-3 sp; repeat from ★ 2 times **more**, then repeat from † to † once; join with slip st to first sc: 364 sc and 364 sps.

Rnd 2: Ch 1, turn; sc in same st, (ch 1, sc in next sc) across to next corner ch-2 sp, (sc, ch 2, sc) in corner ch-2 sp, ★ sc in next sc, (ch 1, sc in next sc) across to next corner ch-2 sp, (sc, ch 2, sc) in corner ch-2 sp; repeat from ★ 2 times **more**; join with slip st to first sc.

Rnd 3: Ch 1, turn; sc in same st, ch 1, skip next sc, (sc, ch 2, sc) in next corner ch-2 sp, ch 1, skip next sc, ★ (sc in next sc, ch 1) across to within one sc of next corner ch-2 sp, skip next sc, (sc, ch 2, sc) in corner ch-2 sp, ch 1, skip next sc; repeat from ★ 2 times **more**, (sc in next sc, ch 1) across; join with slip st to first sc.

Rnd 4: Turn; ★ (slip st in next ch-1 sp, ch 1) across to next corner ch-2 sp, (slip st, ch 2, slip st) in corner ch-2 sp, ch 1; repeat from ★ around, slip st in last ch-1 sp, ch 1; join with slip st to first slip st, finish off.

Design by Anne Halliday.

81

Bringing the outdoors in

Spending time indoors is so much nicer
when you surround yourself with reminders of
the beautiful outdoors. Sprinkle your home with
our stunning afghans — drape one across your
favorite chair, display another at the foot of the bed,
or pick one to hang on the front porch swing.
With so many enticing choices, you'll want
to make them all to bring the splendor
of nature to every room!

Grandma's Flower Garden

Finished Size: 60½" x 76¾"

MATERIALS

Worsted Weight Yarn:
- Green - 35 ounces, (990 grams, 2,400 yards)
- Lt Purple - 5 ounces, (140 grams, 345 yards)
- Purple - 5 ounces, (140 grams, 345 yards)
- Rose - 5 ounces, (140 grams, 345 yards)
- Dk Rose - 5 ounces, (140 grams, 345 yards)
- Blue - 5 ounces, (140 grams, 345 yards)
- Violet - 5 ounces, (140 grams, 345 yards)
- Lt Violet - 4 ounces, (110 grams, 275 yards)
- Lt Blue - 4 ounces, (110 grams, 275 yards)

Crochet hook, size G (4.00 mm) **or** size needed for gauge

Yarn needle

GAUGE SWATCH:

3½" (straight edge to straight edge)
Work same as Motif.

MOTIF

Referring to Key, make the number of Motifs specified in the colors indicated.

Ch 5; join with slip st to form a ring.

Rnd 1 (Right side)**:** Ch 3 **(counts as first dc, now and throughout)**, 17 dc in ring; join with slip st to first dc: 18 dc.

Note: Loop a short piece of yarn around any stitch to mark Rnd 1 as **right** side.

Rnd 2: Ch 3, 2 dc in next dc, dc in next dc, ch 1, ★ dc in next dc, 2 dc in next dc, dc in next dc, ch 1; repeat from ★ around; join with slip st to first dc: 24 dc and 6 ch-1 sps.

Rnd 3: Ch 3, 2 dc in each of next 2 dc, dc in next dc, ch 2, ★ dc in next dc, 2 dc in each of next 2 dc, dc in next dc, ch 2; repeat from ★ around; join with slip st to first dc, finish off: 36 dc and 6 ch-2 sps.

ASSEMBLY

Using Placement Diagram as a guide, with matching colors, and working through **inside** loops only, whipstitch Motifs together **(Fig. 9b, page 144)**, beginning in second ch of first corner ch-2 and ending in first ch of next corner ch-2.

PLACEMENT DIAGRAM

KEY

- ■ - **Green** (Make 183)
- □ - **Lt Purple** (Make 32)
- ■ - **Purple** (Make 29)
- □ - **Rose** (Make 27)
- ■ - **Dk Rose** (Make 32)
- □ - **Lt Blue** (Make 22)
- ■ - **Blue** (Make 27)
- ■ - **Lt Violet** (Make 22)
- ■ - **Violet** (Make 25)

EDGING

With **right** side facing, join Green with slip st in last dc on any Motif; ch 1, sc in same st, skipping sps on either side of joinings, sc in next dc, ch 2, sc in top of sc just made **(Fig. 7, page 143)**, ★ sc in next 2 sts, ch 2, sc in top of last sc made; repeat from ★ around; join with slip st to first sc, finish off.

Design by Jennie Black.

REMEMBER THOSE GLORIOUS DAYS
OF MEANDERING THROUGH GRANDMA'S
FLOWER GARDEN? RECAPTURE THE MEMORIES
WITH THIS VIVID THROW INSPIRED BY
AN OLD-FASHIONED QUILT.

Timeless Treasure

Finished Size: 49" x 65"

MATERIALS
Worsted Weight Brushed Acrylic Yarn:
Tan - 28 ounces, (800 grams, 1,260 yards)
Green - 28 ounces, (800 grams, 1,260 yards)
Rose - 9 ounces, (260 grams, 405 yards)
Crochet hook, size H (5.00 mm) **or** size needed for gauge
Yarn needle

GAUGE: Each Square = 8"

STITCH GUIDE

> **FRONT POST TREBLE CROCHET**
> *(abbreviated FPtr)*
> YO twice, insert hook from **front** to **back** around post of st indicated **(Fig. 4, page 143)**, YO and pull up a loop (4 loops on hook), (YO and draw through 2 loops on hook) 3 times. Skip st behind FPtr.

SQUARE (Make 48)
Rnd 1 (Right side): With Tan, ch 4, 11 dc in fourth ch from hook **(3 skipped chs count as first dc)**; join with slip st to first dc: 12 dc.

Note: Loop a short piece of yarn around any stitch to mark Rnd 1 as **right** side.

Rnd 2: Ch 3 **(counts as first dc, now and throughout)**, dc in same st, 2 dc in each dc around; join with slip st to first dc, finish off: 24 dc.

Rnd 3: With **right** side facing, join Green with slip st in any dc; ch 3, dc in next dc, work FPtr around dc on Rnd 1 **below** dc just made, ★ dc in next 2 dc, work FPtr around dc on Rnd 1 **below** last dc made; repeat from ★ around; join with slip st to first dc, finish off: 12 FPtr.

Rnd 4: With **right** side facing, join Rose with slip st in sp **between** any 2 dc **(Fig. 5, page 143)**; ch 3, 2 dc in same sp, skip next 3 sts, 3 dc in sp **before** next dc, skip next 3 sts, (4 dc, ch 2, 4 dc) in sp **before** next dc, skip next 3 sts, ★ (3 dc in sp **before** next dc, skip next 3 sts) twice, (4 dc, ch 2, 4 dc) in sp **before** next dc, skip next 3 sts; repeat from ★ around; join with slip st to first dc, finish off: 56 dc.

Rnd 5: With **right** side facing, join Green with slip st in any corner ch-2 sp; ch 3, (4 dc, ch 2, 5 dc) in same sp, (3 dc in sp **before** next 3-dc group) twice, 3 dc in sp **before** next 4-dc group, ★ (5 dc, ch 2, 5 dc) in next ch-2 sp, (3 dc in sp **before** next 3-dc group) twice, 3 dc in sp **before** next 4-dc group; repeat from ★ around; join with slip st to first dc, finish off: 76 dc.

Rnd 6: With **right** side facing, join Tan with sc in any corner ch-2 sp **(see Joining With Sc, page 142)**; 2 sc in same sp, working in Back Loops Only **(Fig. 2, page 143)**, sc in each dc around working 3 sc in each corner ch-2 sp; join with slip st to first sc, finish off: 88 sc.

Rnd 7: With **right** side facing and working in Back Loops Only, join Green with slip st in center sc of any corner 3-sc group; ch 3, 4 dc in same st, dc in each sc around working 5 dc in center sc of each corner 3-sc group; join with slip st to first dc, finish off: 104 dc.

Rnd 8: With **right** side facing and working in Back Loops Only, join Tan with slip st in center dc of any corner 5-dc group; ch 3, (2 dc, ch 1, 3 dc) in same st, dc in each dc around working (3 dc, ch 1, 3 dc) in center dc of each corner 5-dc group; join with slip st to first dc, finish off: 124 dc.

ASSEMBLY
With Tan, whipstitch Squares together forming 6 vertical strips of 8 Squares each **(Fig. 9b, page 144)**, beginning in first corner ch and ending in next corner ch; then whipstitch strips together in same manner.

EDGING
With **right** side facing and working in Back Loops Only, join Tan with slip st in any corner ch; ch 3, (2 dc, ch 1, 3 dc) in same st, dc in each dc around working (3 dc, ch 1, 3 dc) in each corner ch; join with slip st to first dc, finish off.

Design by Jan Hatfield.

Finished Size: 48" x 68"

MATERIALS
Worsted Weight Yarn:
37 ounces, (1,050 grams, 2,430 yards)
Crochet hook, size I (5.50 mm) **or** size needed for gauge
Yarn needle

GAUGE SWATCH: 6¹/₂" square
Work same as Square.

STITCH GUIDE

TREBLE CROCHET (abbreviated tr)
YO twice, insert hook in sp indicated, YO and pull up a loop (4 loops on hook), (YO and draw through 2 loops on hook) 3 times.

CLUSTER
Ch 3, dc in third ch from hook, ch 4, dc in third ch from hook.

SQUARE (Make 70)
Rnd 1 (Right side): Ch 5, (dc, ch 1) 7 times in fifth ch from hook; join with slip st to fourth ch of beginning ch-5: 8 ch-1 sps.

Note: Loop a short piece of yarn around any stitch to mark Rnd 1 as **right** side.

Rnd 2: Work Cluster, slip st in first ch-1 sp, work Cluster, ★ slip st in next dc, work Cluster, slip st in next ch-1 sp, work Cluster; repeat from ★ around; join with slip st at base of first Cluster: 16 Clusters.

Rnd 3: Slip st across to center of first Cluster, ch 1, sc in same sp, ch 2, (sc in center of next Cluster, ch 2) twice, (sc, ch 3, sc) in center of next Cluster (corner made), ch 2, ★ (sc in center of next Cluster, ch 2) 3 times, (sc, ch 3, sc) in center of next Cluster (corner made), ch 2; repeat from ★ around; join with slip st to first sc: 20 sps.

Rnd 4: Slip st in first ch-2 sp, ch 1, sc in same sp, ch 4, sc in next ch-2 sp, ch 1, skip next ch-2 sp, (tr, ch 1) 7 times in corner ch-3 sp, skip next ch-2 sp, ★ sc in next ch-2 sp, ch 4, sc in next ch-2 sp, ch 1, skip next ch-2 sp, (tr, ch 1) 7 times

in corner ch-3 sp, skip next ch-2 sp; repeat from ★ around; join with slip st to first sc.

Rnd 5: Slip st in first 2 chs, ch 1, sc in same ch-4 sp, ★ † (ch 5, skip next ch-1 sp, sc in next ch-1 sp) twice, ch 7, sc in next ch-1 sp (corner made), ch 5, skip next ch-1 sp, sc in next ch-1 sp, ch 5, skip next ch-1 sp †, sc in next ch-4 sp; repeat from ★ 2 times **more**, then repeat from † to † once; join with slip st to first sc: 20 sps.

Rnd 6: Slip st in first 2 chs, ch 3 **(counts as first dc, now and throughout)**, 2 dc in same ch-5 sp, ch 1, 3 dc in next ch-5 sp, ch 1, (3 dc, ch 3, 3 dc) in next corner ch-7 sp, ch 1, ★ (3 dc in next ch-5 sp, ch 1) 4 times, (3 dc, ch 3, 3 dc) in next corner ch-7 sp, ch 1; repeat from ★ 2 times **more**, (3 dc in next ch-5 sp, ch 1) twice; join with slip st to first dc, finish off: 20 ch-1 sps.

ASSEMBLY
Whipstitch Squares together forming 7 vertical strips of 10 Squares each **(Fig. 9a, page 144)**, beginning in center ch of first corner ch-3 and ending in center ch of next corner ch-3; then whipstitch strips together in same manner.

EDGING
Rnd 1: With **right** side facing, join yarn with slip st in any corner ch-3 sp; ch 3, (dc, ch 2, 2 dc) in same sp, ★ † dc in next 3 dc, (ch 1, dc in next 3 dc) 5 times, [ch 1, dc in joining, (ch 1, dc in next 3 dc) 6 times] across to next corner ch-3 sp †, (2 dc, ch 3, 2 dc) in corner ch-3 sp; repeat from ★ 2 times **more**, then repeat from † to † once; join with slip st to first dc.

Rnd 2: Slip st in next dc and next corner ch-3 sp, ch 6, dc in same sp, ★ † ch 1, dc in next dc, ch 1, skip next dc, (dc in next dc, ch 1, skip next dc, dc in next dc, ch 1) 6 times, [dc in next dc, ch 1, (dc in next dc, ch 1, skip next dc, dc in next dc, ch 1) 6 times] across to within 2 dc of next corner ch-3 sp, skip next dc, dc in next dc, ch 1 †, (dc, ch 3, dc) in corner ch-3 sp; repeat from ★ 2 times **more**, then repeat from † to † once; join with slip st to third ch of beginning ch-6, do **not** finish off.

Continued on page 129.

Finished Size: 47" x 65"

MATERIALS

Worsted Weight Yarn:
Ecru - 19 ounces, (540 grams, 1,305 yards)
Lt Purple - 15¹/₂ ounces,
  (440 grams, 1,045 yards)
Purple - 7¹/₄ ounces, (210 grams, 500 yards)
Green - 5 ounces, (140 grams, 345 yards)
Crochet hook, size J (6.00 mm) **or** size needed
  for gauge

GAUGE: In pattern, 14 hdc = 4"; Rows 8-14 = 3¹/₄"

Gauge Swatch: 4"w x 3¹/₂"h
With Green, ch 15 **loosely**.
Row 1: Hdc in third ch from hook (**2 skipped chs count as first hdc**) and in each ch across: 14 hdc.
Rows 2-7: Ch 2 (**counts as first hdc**), turn; hdc in next hdc and in each hdc across.
Finish off.

Each row is worked across length of Afghan.

STITCH GUIDE

CLUSTER (uses one st)
★ YO, insert hook in st indicated, YO and pull up a loop even with loop on hook; repeat from ★ once **more**, YO and draw through all 5 loops on hook.

BEGINNING 2-PETAL GROUP (uses one hdc)
Work Cluster in next hdc, ch 3, work Cluster in third ch from hook.

2-PETAL GROUP (uses next 2 hdc)
Ch 4, YO, insert hook in third ch from hook, YO and pull up a loop even with loop on hook (3 loops on hook), YO, insert hook in same ch, YO and pull up a loop even with loop on hook (5 loops on hook), YO, skip next hdc, insert hook in next hdc, YO and pull up a loop even with loop on hook, YO, insert hook in same st, YO and pull up a loop even with loop on hook (9 loops on hook), YO and draw through all 9 loops on hook.

BEGINNING 4-PETAL GROUP
(uses next 5 hdc)
YO, insert hook in third ch from hook, YO and pull up a loop even with loop on hook (3 loops on hook), YO, insert hook in same ch, YO and pull up a loop even with loop on hook (5 loops on hook), † YO, insert hook in **next** hdc, YO and pull up a loop even with loop on hook, YO, insert hook in **same** st, YO and pull up a loop even with loop on hook † (9 loops on hook), skip next 3 hdc, repeat from † to † once (13 loops on hook), YO and draw through all 13 loops on hook, ch 3, work Cluster in third ch from hook.

4-PETAL GROUP (uses next 6 hdc)
YO, insert hook in third ch from hook, YO and pull up a loop even with loop on hook (3 loops on hook), YO, insert hook in same ch, YO and pull up a loop even with loop on hook (5 loops on hook), YO, skip next hdc, † insert hook in **next** hdc, YO and pull up a loop even with loop on hook, YO, insert hook in **same** st, YO and pull up a loop even with loop on hook † (9 loops on hook), YO, skip next 3 hdc, repeat from † to † once (13 loops on hook), YO and draw through all 13 loops on hook, ch 3, work Cluster in third ch from hook.

PUFF STITCH (*abbreviated Puff St*)
★ YO, insert hook in st indicated, YO and pull up a loop even with loop on hook; repeat from ★ 2 times **more** (7 loops on hook), YO and draw through all 7 loops on hook.

AFGHAN

Foundation Row (Right side)**:** With Lt Purple, ★ ch 4, work Cluster in third ch from hook, ch 3, work Cluster in top of last Cluster made (**Fig. 7, page 143**); repeat from ★ 37 times **more**, do **not** finish off: 76 Clusters.

Note: Loop a short piece of yarn around any stitch to mark Foundation Row as **right** side.

Continued on page 130.

Pretty Posies

Finished Size: 45¹/₂" x 60¹/₂"

MATERIALS
Worsted Weight Yarn:
    White - 17 ounces, (480 grams, 1,115 yards)
    Green - 10¹/₂ ounces, (300 grams, 690 yards)
    Lt Rose - 7¹/₂ ounces, (210 grams, 490 yards)
    Rose - 3¹/₂ ounces, (100 grams, 230 yards)
Crochet hook, size I (5.50 mm) **or** size needed
    for gauge

GAUGE: Each Strip = 6¹/₂" wide

Gauge Swatch: 1³/₄" square
With Rose, ch 4; join with slip st to form a ring.
Rnd 1 (Right side)**:** Ch 3 **(counts as first dc)**, [dc, ch 2, (3 dc, ch 2) 3 times, dc] in ring; join with slip st to first dc, finish off.

STITCH GUIDE

TREBLE CROCHET *(abbreviated tr)*
YO twice, insert hook in sp indicated, YO and pull up a loop (4 loops on hook), (YO and draw through 2 loops on hook) 3 times.

LONG SINGLE CROCHET *(abbreviated LSC)*
Insert hook in st indicated, YO and pull up a loop even with loop on hook, YO and draw through both loops on hook.

JOINING
Drop loop from hook, insert hook in st indicated, hook dropped look and draw through.

DECREASE
Pull up a loop in same sp as last sc made, skip joining, pull up a loop in next ch-1 sp, YO and draw through both loops on hook **(counts as one sc)**.

FIRST STRIP
With Rose, ch 4; join with slip st to form a ring.

Foundation (Right side)**:** Ch 3 **(counts as first dc, now and throughout)**, dc in ring, place marker around dc just made to mark **right** side and for st placement, ch 2, [(3 dc, ch 2) 3 times, dc] in ring; join with slip st to first dc **(first Motif made)**, ★ ch 14, slip st in fourth ch from hook to form a ring; ch 3, working over remaining ch-10, (dc, ch 2, 3 dc, ch 2, 2 dc) in ring, skip remaining chs of ch-10, (dc, ch 2, 3 dc, ch 2, dc) in same ring; join with slip st to first dc; repeat from ★ 11 times **more**; finish off: 13 Motifs.

Rnd 1: With **right** side facing, join White with dc in marked dc on Foundation **(see Joining With Dc, page 142)**; (3 dc, ch 1, 3 dc) in next ch-2 sp, dc in next dc, ch 1, [skip next dc, dc in next dc, (3 dc, ch 1, 3 dc) in next ch-2 sp, dc in next dc, ch 1] 3 times, skip next ch **between** Motifs, sc in next 5 chs, ch 1, keeping remaining chs **behind** Motifs, ★ dc in third dc of next 3-dc group on next Motif, (3 dc, ch 1, 3 dc) in next ch-2 sp, dc in next dc, ch 1, skip next dc, dc in next dc, (3 dc, ch 1, 3 dc) in next ch-2 sp, dc in next dc, ch 1, skip next ch **between** Motifs, sc in next 5 chs, ch 1; repeat from ★ across to last Motif, place marker around last ch-1 made for st placement, dc in third dc of next 3-dc group on last Motif, (3 dc, ch 1, 3 dc) in next ch-2 sp, dc in next dc, [ch 1, skip next dc, dc in next dc, (3 dc, ch 1, 3 dc) in next ch-2 sp, dc in next dc] 3 times, slip st in marked ch-1 on opposite side, sc in free loop of ch at base of next 5 sc **(Fig. 3b, page 143)**, slip st in next ch-1 on opposite side, † dc in last dc of next 3-dc group on next Motif, (3 dc, ch 1, 3 dc) in next ch-2 sp, dc in next dc, ch 1, skip next dc, dc in next dc, (3 dc, ch 1, 3 dc) in next ch-2 sp, dc in next dc, slip st in next ch-1 on opposite side, sc in free loop of ch at base of next 5 sc, slip st in next ch-1 on opposite side †; repeat from † to † across; join with slip st to first dc, finish off.

Continued on page 131.

FOR A BEAUTIFUL ACCENT IN A LITTLE GIRL'S ROOM, OUR PRETTY POSY BLANKET IS ALIVE WITH ENGAGING HUES OF ROSE AND GREEN. THE LACY LOOK BETWEEN THE STRIPS IS CREATED WHEN THE SCALLOPED EDGES ARE JOINED PEAK TO PEAK.

Roses on Lace

Finished Size: 48" x 58"

MATERIALS

Worsted Weight Yarn:
  Ecru - 41 ounces, (1,160 grams, 2,315 yards)
  Green - 5 ounces, (140 grams, 285 yards)
  Rose - 3 ounces, (90 grams, 170 yards)
  Dk Rose - 3 ounces, (90 grams, 170 yards)
  Purple - 3 ounces, (90 grams, 170 yards)
  Blue - 3 ounces, (90 grams, 170 yards)
Crochet hook, size G (4.00 mm) **or** size needed for gauge

GAUGE: Each Square = 8"

Gauge Swatch: 3½" diameter
Work same as Rose.

STITCH GUIDE

> **CLUSTER** (uses one sp)
> ★ YO twice, insert hook in ch-5 sp indicated, YO and pull up a loop, (YO and draw through 2 loops on hook) twice; repeat from ★ 3 times **more**, YO and draw through all 5 loops on hook.

SQUARE (Make 30)

Make the number of Squares indicated through Inner Petals in each of the following colors:
Rose - 7, Dk Rose - 8, Purple - 7, and Blue - 8.

ROSE

With color indicated, ch 4; join with slip st to form a ring.

Rnd 1 (Right side)**:** Ch 6 (**counts as first dc plus ch 3**), (dc in ring, ch 3) 7 times; join with slip st to first dc: 8 ch-3 sps.

Note: Loop a short piece of yarn around any stitch to mark Rnd 1 as **right** side.

Rnd 2: Ch 1, (sc, hdc, dc, hdc, sc) in each ch-3 sp around; join with slip st to first sc: 8 petals.

Rnd 3: Ch 1, working **behind** petals and around posts of dc in Rnd 1, sc around first dc, ch 4, (sc around next dc, ch 4) around; join with slip st to first sc: 8 ch-4 sps.

Rnd 4: Ch 1, (sc, hdc, 3 dc, hdc, sc) in each ch-4 sp around; join with slip st to first sc: 8 petals.

Rnd 5: Ch 1, working **behind** petals and around posts of sc on Rnd 3, sc around first sc, ch 5, (sc around next sc, ch 5) around; join with slip st to first sc, finish off: 8 ch-5 sps.

INNER PETALS

Rnd 1: With **right** side facing and working around posts of dc on Rnd 1 (**below** sc on Rnd 3), join same color yarn with sc around post of any dc **(see Joining With Sc, page 142)**; ch 5, (sc around next dc, ch 5) around; join with slip st to first sc: 8 ch-5 sps.

Rnd 2: Ch 1, 5 sc in each ch-5 sp around; join with slip st to first sc, finish off: 40 sc.

BORDER

Rnd 1: With **right** side of Rose facing, join Green with slip st in any ch-5 sp on Rnd 5; ch 10, work (Cluster, ch 5, Cluster) in next ch-5 sp, ch 10, ★ slip st in next ch-5 sp, ch 10, work (Cluster, ch 5, Cluster) in next ch-5 sp, ch 10; repeat from ★ 2 times **more**; join with slip st to first slip st, finish off: 12 sps.

Rnd 2: With **right** side facing, join Ecru with sc in any ch-5 sp; 4 sc in same sp, ★ † 15 sc in next ch-10 sp, working **around** next slip st, sc in ch-5 sp on Rnd 5 of Rose, 8 sc in next ch-10 sp, drop loop from hook, insert hook from **front** to **back** in eighth sc worked in previous ch-10 sp, hook dropped loop and pull through, ch 1, 7 sc in same sp †, 9 sc in next ch-5 sp; repeat from ★ 2 times **more**, then repeat from † to † once, 4 sc in same sp as first sc; join with slip st to first sc, do **not** finish off.

Continued on page 132.

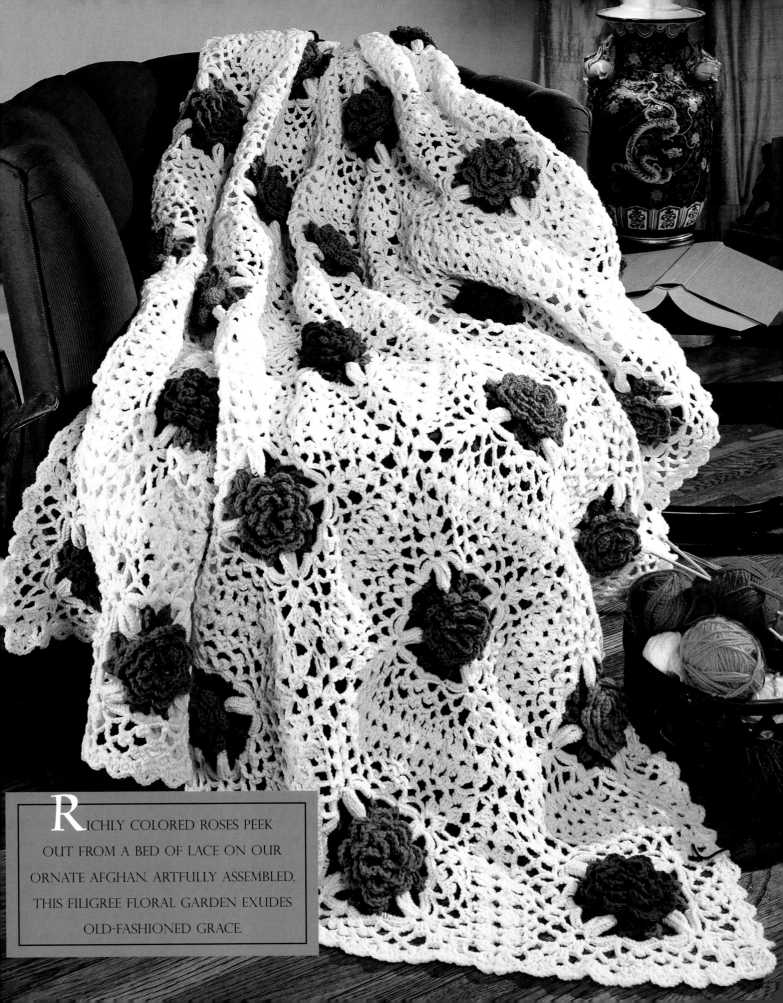

RICHLY COLORED ROSES PEEK
OUT FROM A BED OF LACE ON OUR
ORNATE AFGHAN. ARTFULLY ASSEMBLED,
THIS FILIGREE FLORAL GARDEN EXUDES
OLD-FASHIONED GRACE.

Love Letters

Finished Size: 50" x 67"

MATERIALS

Worsted Weight Yarn:
Ecru - 26 ounces, (740 grams, 1,785 yards)
Green - 12¹/₂ ounces, (360 grams, 860 yards)
Crochet hook, size I (5.50 mm) **or** size needed
for gauge
Yarn needle

GAUGE: Each Strip = 5¹/₂" wide

Gauge Swatch: 2¹/₂"w x 6"h
Foundation Row: (Ch 4, tr in fourth ch from hook
to form a ring) 4 times.
Rnd 1: Slip st in first ring, ch 5, (tr in same ring,
ch 1) 5 times, sc in next ring, ch 3, sc in next ring,
ch 1, (tr, ch 1) 11 times in next ring; working on
opposite side of Foundation Row, sc in next ring,
ch 3, sc in next ring, ch 1, (tr, ch 1) 5 times in
same ring as first tr; join with slip st to fourth ch of
beginning ch-5, finish off.

STITCH GUIDE

TREBLE CROCHET (abbreviated tr)
YO twice, insert hook in st or sp indicated, YO
and pull up a loop (4 loops on hook), (YO and
draw through 2 loops on hook) 3 times.

CLUSTER
YO, insert hook in third ch from hook, YO and
pull up a loop, YO and draw through 2 loops
on hook, YO, insert hook in same ch, YO and
pull up a loop, YO and draw through 2 loops
on hook, YO and draw through all 3 loops on
hook.

DECREASE (uses next 3 sts)
YO twice, insert hook in next dc, YO and pull
up a loop, (YO and draw through 2 loops on
hook) twice, YO twice, skip next sc, insert
hook in next dc, YO and pull up a loop, (YO
and draw through 2 loops on hook) twice, YO
and draw through all 3 loops on hook.

STRIP (Make 9)

Foundation Row: With Ecru, (ch 4, tr in fourth ch
from hook to form a ring) 58 times. 61

Rnd 1 (Right side): Slip st in first ring, ch 5, (tr in
same ring, ch 1) 5 times, sc in next ring, ch 3, sc
in next ring, ch 1, ★ (tr, ch 1) 5 times in next ring,
sc in next ring, ch 3, sc in next ring, ch 1; repeat
from ★ across to last ring, (tr, ch 1) 11 times in last
ring; working on opposite side of Foundation Row,
[sc in next ring, ch 3, sc in next ring, ch 1, (tr,
ch 1) 5 times in next ring] across; join with slip st
to fourth ch of beginning ch-5: 278 sts and
278 sps.

Note: Loop a short piece of yarn around any stitch
to mark Rnd 1 as **right** side.

Rnd 2: Ch 6 **(counts as first dc plus ch 3)**, **turn**;
work Cluster, † dc in next tr, (ch 3, work Cluster,
dc in next tr) 4 times, skip next ch-1 sp, sc in next
ch-3 sp, skip next ch-1 sp †, repeat from † to †
18 times **more**, dc in next tr, (ch 3, work Cluster,
dc in next tr) 10 times, skip next ch-1 sp, sc in
next ch-3 sp, skip next ch-1 sp, repeat from † to †
18 times, (dc in next tr, ch 3, work Cluster) 5
times; join with slip st to first dc, finish off:
202 dc.

Rnd 3: With **right** side facing, join Green with
slip st in same st as joining; ch 4, dc in same st,
ch 1, skip next Cluster, (dc, ch 1) twice in next dc,
skip next Cluster, † (dc, ch 2) twice in next dc,
skip next Cluster, sc in next dc, ★ ch 2, skip next
Cluster, dc in next dc, ch 2, skip next Cluster,
decrease, ch 2, skip next Cluster, dc in next dc,
ch 2, skip next Cluster, sc in next dc; repeat from
★ 18 times **more**, ch 2, skip next Cluster, (dc,
ch 2, dc) in next dc, place marker around last ch-2
made for st placement, ch 1, skip next Cluster †,
[(dc, ch 1) twice in next dc, skip next Cluster] 3
times, repeat from † to † once, (dc, ch 1) twice in
next dc, skip last Cluster; join with slip st to third
ch of beginning ch-4, do **not** finish off: 174 sts and
174 sps.

Continued on page 133.

LIKE SWEET NOTHINGS WHISPERED IN YOUR EAR, THIS COZY WRAP REFLECTS SENTIMENTS OF LOVE. WORKED IN LACY STRIPS, THE INTRIGUING AFGHAN WOULD LOOK BECOMING IN ANY COLOR COMBINATION.

Lilac Lace

Finished Size: 45" x 60"

MATERIALS
Worsted Weight Yarn:
   49$\frac{1}{2}$ ounces, (1,410 grams, 2,800 yards)
Crochet hook, size H (5.00 mm) **or** size needed
   for gauge
Yarn needle

GAUGE: Each Strip = 5$\frac{1}{2}$" wide

Gauge Swatch: 3$\frac{1}{2}$" square
Work same as First Strip Center through Row 6.

STITCH GUIDE

V-ST
(Dc, ch 1, dc) in st indicated.

FRONT POPCORN
5 Dc in ch-1 sp indicated, drop loop from hook, insert hook from **front** to **back** in first dc of 5-dc group, hook dropped loop and draw through.

BACK POPCORN
5 Dc in ch-1 sp indicated, drop loop from hook, insert hook from **back** to **front** in first dc of 5-dc group, hook dropped loop and draw through.

LINKED BACK POST TREBLE CROCHET
   (abbreviated LBPtr)
YO twice, working **behind** sts on previous row, insert hook from **back** to **front** around post of dc indicated **(Fig. 4, page 143)**, YO and pull up a loop (4 loops on hook), YO and draw through 2 loops on hook, insert hook in ch indicated, YO and pull up a loop (4 loops on hook), YO and draw through 3 loops on hook, YO and draw through remaining 2 loops on hook.

LINKED FRONT POST TREBLE CROCHET
   (abbreviated LFPtr)
YO twice, working in front of sts on previous row, insert hook from **front** to **back** around post of dc indicated **(Fig. 4, page 143)**, YO and pull up a loop (4 loops on hook), YO and draw through 2 loops on hook, keeping

working yarn behind hook, insert hook in ch indicated, YO and pull up a loop (4 loops on hook), YO and draw through 3 loops on hook, YO and draw through remaining 2 loops on hook.

FIRST STRIP
CENTER
Ch 12.

Row 1: Sc in second ch from hook and in next 2 chs, ch 3, skip next 2 chs, work V-St in next ch, ch 3, skip next 2 chs, sc in last 3 chs: 8 sts and 3 sps.

Row 2 (Right side)**:** Ch 3 **(counts as first dc, now and throughout)**, turn; 3 dc in next ch-3 sp, ch 3, work Front Popcorn in next ch-1 sp, ch 3, 3 dc in next ch-3 sp, skip next 2 sc, dc in last sc: 9 sts and 2 ch-3 sps.

Note: Loop a short piece of yarn around any stitch to mark Row 2 as **right** side and bottom edge.

Row 3: Ch 4 **(counts as first dc plus ch 1, now and throughout)**, turn; skip next 3 dc, work LBPtr around first dc of V-St 2 rows **below** and in first ch of next ch-3, (hdc, sc) in same ch-3 sp, sc in next Popcorn, (sc, hdc) in next ch-3 sp, work LBPtr around next dc of same V-St 2 rows **below** and in third ch of same ch-3, ch 1, skip next 3 dc, dc in last dc: 9 sts and 2 ch-1 sps.

Row 4: Ch 1, turn; sc in first dc, sc in next ch and in next LBPtr, ch 3, skip next 2 sts, work V-St in next sc, ch 3, skip next 2 sts, sc in next LBPtr, sc in next ch and in last dc: 8 sts and 3 sps.

Row 5: Ch 3, turn; 3 dc in next ch-3 sp, ch 3, work Back Popcorn in next ch-1 sp, ch 3, 3 dc in next ch-3 sp, skip next 2 sc, dc in last sc.

Row 6: Ch 4, turn; skip next 3 dc, work LFPtr around first dc of V-St 2 rows **below** and in first ch of next ch-3, (hdc, sc) in same ch-3 sp, sc in next Popcorn, (sc, hdc) in next ch-3 sp, work LFPtr around next dc of same V-St 2 rows **below** and in third ch of same ch-3, ch 1, skip next 3 dc, dc in last dc; do **not** finish off: 9 sts and 2 ch-1 sps.

Continued on page 134.

TRADITIONAL IN DESIGN, OUR DISTINCTIVE
AFGHAN DELIVERS A LEGACY OF DELIGHT.
THE LACY CREATION IS AS PRETTY AS
A PROFUSION OF LILACS.

Finished Size: 50½" x 67"

MATERIALS
Brushed Acrylic Worsted Weight Yarn:
43 ounces, (1,220 grams, 2,180 yards)
Crochet hook, size I (5.50 mm) **or** size needed
for gauge
Yarn needle

GAUGE: First Motif = 5½" diameter

Gauge Swatch: 3½" diameter
Work same as First Motif through Rnd 2.

STITCH GUIDE

BEGINNING DOUBLE CROCHET CLUSTER
(abbreviated Beginning dc Cluster)
(uses one sp)
Ch 2, ★ YO, insert hook in sp indicated, YO
and pull up a loop, YO and draw through
2 loops on hook; repeat from ★ once **more**,
YO and draw through all 3 loops on hook.

DOUBLE CROCHET CLUSTER
(abbreviated dc Cluster) (uses one sp)
★ YO, insert hook in sp indicated, YO and pull
up a loop, YO and draw through 2 loops on
hook; repeat from ★ 2 times **more**, YO and
draw through all 4 loops on hook.

BEGINNING TREBLE CROCHET CLUSTER
(abbreviated Beginning tr Cluster)
(uses one sp)
Ch 3, ★ YO twice, insert hook in **same** sp, YO
and pull up a loop, (YO and draw through
2 loops on hook) twice; repeat from ★ once
more, YO and draw through all 3 loops on
hook.

TREBLE CROCHET CLUSTER
(abbreviated tr Cluster) (uses one ch-3 sp)
★ YO twice, insert hook in sp indicated, YO
and pull up a loop, (YO and draw through
2 loops on hook) twice; repeat from ★ 2 times
more, YO and draw through all 4 loops on
hook.

FIRST MOTIF
Ch 4; join with slip st to form a ring.

Rnd 1 (Right side)**:** Ch 1, (sc in ring, ch 3) 8 times;
join with slip st to first sc: 8 ch-3 sps.

Note: Loop a short piece of yarn around any stitch
to mark Rnd 1 as **right** side.

Rnd 2: Slip st in first ch-3 sp, work Beginning
tr Cluster, ch 4, (work tr Cluster in next ch-3 sp,
ch 4) around; join with slip st to top of Beginning
tr Cluster: 8 tr Clusters and 8 ch-4 sps.

Rnd 3: Ch 4 **(counts as first dc plus ch 1)**, dc in
same st, (dc, ch 1, dc) in each ch-4 sp and in each
tr Cluster around; join with slip st to first dc:
16 ch-1 sps.

Rnd 4: Slip st in first ch-1 sp, ch 1, sc in same sp,
ch 5, (sc in next ch-1 sp, ch 5) around; join with
slip st to first sc, finish off: 16 ch-5 sps.

ADDITIONAL MOTIFS
The method used to connect the Motifs is a
no-sew joining also known as "join-as-you-go".
After the First Motif is made, each remaining Motif
is worked through Rnd 3, then crocheted together
as Rnd 4 is worked.

Work same as First Motif through Rnd 3:
16 ch-1 sps.

Rnd 4 (Joining rnd)**:** Work One or Two Side Joining
(Fig. 10, page 144), arranging Motifs into
7 vertical rows of 10 Motifs each.

ONE SIDE JOINING
Rnd 4 (Joining rnd)**:** Slip st in first ch-1 sp, ch 1, sc
in same sp, (ch 5, sc in next ch-1 sp) 13 times,
ch 2, holding Motifs with **wrong** sides together, sc
in corresponding ch-5 sp on **adjacent Motif**, ch 2,
★ sc in next ch-1 sp on **new Motif**, ch 2, sc in
next ch-5 sp on **adjacent Motif**, ch 2; repeat
from ★ once **more**; join with slip st to first sc on
new Motif, finish off.

Continued on page 134

LACY CIRCULAR MOTIFS WITH
FLORAL CENTERS HIGHLIGHT THIS
EXQUISITE AFGHAN. CHAIN LOOPS
AND SHELL CLUSTERS FORM THE
DEEP, INTRICATE EDGING.

Finished Size: 47" x 63"

MATERIALS

Worsted Weight Yarn:
Ecru - 40 ounces, (1,140 grams, 2,260 yards)
Scraps - 27 ounces,
(770 grams, 1,525 yards) **total**
Note: We used 8 different colors.
Crochet hook, size I (5.50 mm) **or** size needed
for gauge
Yarn needle

GAUGE: Each Motif = 4$\frac{1}{2}$"
(straight edge to straight edge)

Gauge Swatch: 1$\frac{3}{4}$" diameter
Work same as Motif through Rnd 1.

STITCH GUIDE

TREBLE CROCHET *(abbreviated tr)*
YO twice, insert hook in st indicated, YO and
pull up a loop (4 loops on hook), (YO and
draw through 2 loops on hook) 3 times.

CLUSTER
Ch 3, YO, insert hook in third ch from hook,
YO and pull up a loop, YO and draw through
2 loops on hook, YO, insert hook in **same** ch,
YO and pull up a loop, YO and draw through
2 loops on hook, YO and draw through all
3 loops on hook.

DECREASE (uses 2 sps)
† YO, insert hook in next sp, YO and pull up a
loop, YO and draw through 2 loops on hook †,
skip next joining, repeat from † to † once, YO
and draw through all 3 loops on hook.

MOTIF (Make 143)

Rnd 1 (Right side): With Ecru, ch 5, (dc, ch 1) 7
times in fifth ch from hook (**4 skipped chs count
as first dc plus ch 1**); join with slip st to first dc,
finish off: 8 dc and 8 ch-1 sps.

Note: Loop a short piece of yarn around any stitch
to mark Rnd 1 as **right** side.

Rnd 2: With **wrong** side facing, join color desired
with sc in any dc (*see Joining With Sc, page 142*);
work Cluster, (sc in next dc, work Cluster) around;
join with slip st to first sc, finish off: 8 Clusters and
8 sc.

Rnd 3: With **right** side facing, join Ecru with sc in
any sc; working **behind** next Cluster (*Fig. 6,
page 143*), 2 dc in skipped ch-1 sp one rnd **below**,
★ sc in next sc, working **behind** next Cluster, 2 dc
in skipped ch-1 sp one rnd **below**; repeat from ★
around; join with slip st to first sc, finish off:
24 sts.

Rnd 4: With **wrong** side facing, join color desired
with sc in any st; work Cluster, skip next st, ★ sc
in next st, work Cluster, skip next st; repeat from ★
around; join with slip st to first sc, finish off:
12 Clusters and 12 sc.

Rnd 5: With **right** side facing, join Ecru with dc in
any sc (*see Joining With Dc, page 142*); ch 3, dc
in same st, ★ † working **behind** next Cluster, tr in
skipped st one rnd **below**, dc in next sc, working
behind next Cluster, tr in skipped st one rnd
below †, (dc, ch 3, dc) in next sc; repeat from ★
4 times **more**, then repeat from † to † once; join
with slip st to first dc, finish off: 30 sts and
6 ch-3 sps.

HALF MOTIF (Make 14)

Row 1 (Right side): With Ecru, ch 6, [dc, (ch 3, dc)
twice, ch 1, tr] in sixth ch from hook (**5 skipped
chs count as first tr plus ch 1**): 5 sts and 4 sps.

Note: Mark Row 1 as **right** side.

Row 2: Ch 5 (**counts as first tr plus ch 1, now and
throughout**), turn; dc in next ch-1 sp and in next
dc, ★ (dc, ch 3, dc) in next ch-3 sp, dc in next dc;
repeat from ★ once **more**, dc in next ch-1 sp,
ch 1, tr in last tr: 11 sts and 4 sps.

Row 3: Ch 5, turn; dc in next ch-1 sp and in next
3 dc, ★ (dc, ch 3, dc) in next ch-3 sp, dc in next
3 dc; repeat from ★ once **more**, dc in next
ch-1 sp, ch 1, tr in last tr, finish off: 17 sts and
4 sps.

Continued on page 136.

WITH THE APPEAL OF VINTAGE CHENILLE,
THIS THROW WILL ADD CHARM TO ANY ROOM.
USE SCRAPS IN A WIDE VARIETY OF COLORS
TO CREATE THE VIBRANT BLOOMS.

Adoring Hearts

Finished Size: 46¹/₂" x 59"

MATERIALS
  Worsted Weight Yarn:
    57 ounces, (1,620 grams, 2,755 yards)
  Crochet hook, size I (5.50 mm) **or** size needed
    for gauge
  Yarn needle

GAUGE: Each Square = 6¹/₄"

Gauge Swatch: 3³/₄" square
Work same as Square through Rnd 3.

STITCH GUIDE

HEART ST
(Dc, ch 1) 3 times in Front Loop Only of next dc *(Fig. 2, page 143)*, working from **front** to **back**, slip st around post of dc 2 rnds **below** same st *(Fig. 4, page 143)*, (ch 1, dc) 3 times in Front Loop Only of same st as last dc made.

SQUARE (Make 63)
Ch 5; join with slip st to form a ring.

Rnd 1 (Right side)**:** Ch 6 **(counts as first dc plus ch 3)**, (3 dc in ring, ch 3) 3 times, 2 dc in ring; join with slip st to first dc: 12 dc and 4 ch-3 sps.

Note: Loop a short piece of yarn around any stitch to mark Rnd 1 as **right** side.

Rnd 2: Slip st in first ch-3 sp, ch 1, (sc, ch 3, sc) in same sp, ch 1, skip next dc, sc in next dc, ch 1, ★ (sc, ch 3, sc) in next ch-3 sp, ch 1, skip next dc, sc in next dc, ch 1; repeat from ★ 2 times **more**; join with slip st to first sc: 12 sc and 12 sps.

Rnd 3: Slip st in first ch-3 sp, ch 3 **(counts as first dc, now and throughout)**, (dc, ch 3, 2 dc) in same sp, dc in next sc, (dc in next ch-1 sp and in next sc) twice, ★ (2 dc, ch 3, 2 dc) in next ch-3 sp, dc in next sc, (dc in next ch-1 sp and in next st) twice; repeat from ★ 2 times **more**; join with slip st to first dc: 36 dc and 4 ch-3 sps.

Rnd 4: Slip st in next dc and in next ch-3 sp, ch 1, (sc, ch 3, sc) in same sp, sc in next 3 dc, skip next dc, work Heart St, skip next dc, sc in **both** loops of next 3 dc, ★ (sc, ch 3, sc) in next ch-3 sp, sc in next 3 dc, skip next dc, work Heart St, skip next dc, sc in **both** loops of next 3 sts; repeat from ★ 2 times **more**; join with slip st to first sc: 4 Heart Sts, 32 sc, and 4 ch-3 sps.

Rnd 5: Slip st in first ch-3 sp, ch 1, (sc, ch 3, sc) in same sp, sc in next 4 sc, ch 1, dc in free loop of same st as Heart St *(Fig. 3a, page 143)*, ch 1, sc in next 4 sc, ★ (sc, ch 3, sc) in next ch-3 sp, sc in next 4 sc, ch 1, dc in free loop of same st as Heart St, ch 1, sc in next 4 sc; repeat from ★ 2 times **more**; join with slip st to first sc: 44 sts and 12 sps.

Rnd 6: Slip st in first ch-3 sp, ch 3, (dc, ch 3, 2 dc) in same sp, dc in next sc, (ch 1, skip next sc, dc in next sc) twice, (ch 1, skip next ch-1 sp, dc in next st) twice, (ch 1, skip next sc, dc in next sc) twice, ★ (2 dc, ch 3, 2 dc) in next ch-3 sp, dc in next sc, (ch 1, skip next sc, dc in next sc) twice, (ch 1, skip next ch-1 sp, dc in next st) twice, (ch 1, skip next sc, dc in next st) twice; repeat from ★ 2 times **more**; join with slip st to first dc: 44 dc and 28 sps.

Rnd 7: Ch 1, sc in same st and in next dc, (sc, ch 3, sc) in next corner ch-3 sp, ★ sc in each dc and in each ch-1 sp across to next corner ch-3 sp, (sc, ch 3, sc) in corner ch-3 sp; repeat from ★ 2 times **more**, sc in each dc and in each ch-1 sp across; join with slip st to first sc, finish off: 76 sc and 4 ch-3 sps.

ASSEMBLY
Whipstitch Squares together forming 7 vertical strips of 9 Squares each *(Fig. 9b, page 144)*, beginning in center ch of first corner ch-3 and ending in center ch of next corner ch-3; then whipstitch strips together in same manner.

Continued on page 136.

Rich and luxuriant, our toasty afghan celebrates the exhilarating days of fall — swirling leaves, blooming mums, and chilly breezes. The unique floral designs are made using heart stitches. Long, flowing fringe finishes the top and bottom.

Grandmother's Lace

Finished Size: 50" x 70"

MATERIALS
Worsted Weight Yarn:
  43 ounces, (1,220 grams, 2,950 yards)
Crochet hook, size I (5.50 mm) **or** size needed
  for gauge
Yarn needle

GAUGE: Each Motif = 4³/₄"
        (straight edge to straight edge)

Gauge Swatch: 3¹/₄" diameter
Work same as Motif through Rnd 2.

STITCH GUIDE

TREBLE CROCHET (abbreviated tr)
YO twice, insert hook in sp indicated, YO and
pull up a loop (4 loops on hook), (YO and
draw through 2 loops on hook) 3 times.

BEGINNING CLUSTER (uses next 3 tr)
Ch 2, ★ YO, insert hook in **next** tr, YO and
pull up a loop, YO and draw through 2 loops
on hook; repeat from ★ 2 times **more**, YO and
draw through all 4 loops on hook.

CLUSTER (uses next 4 tr)
★ YO, insert hook in **next** tr, YO and pull up a
loop, YO and draw through 2 loops on hook;
repeat from ★ 3 times **more**, YO and draw
through all 5 loops on hook.

DECREASE (uses next 2 sps)
★ YO, insert hook in **next** sp, YO and pull up
a loop, YO and draw through 2 loops on hook;
repeat from ★ once **more**, YO and draw
through all 3 loops on hook.

MOTIF (Make 162)
Rnd 1 (Right side)**:** Ch 6, (dc, ch 2) 5 times in sixth
ch from hook; join with slip st to fourth ch of
beginning ch-6: 6 ch-2 sps.

Note: Loop a short piece of yarn around any stitch
to mark Rnd 1 as **right** side.

Rnd 2: Slip st in first ch-2 sp, ch 4 **(counts as first
tr)**, 3 tr in same sp, ch 3, (4 tr in next ch-2 sp,
ch 3) around; join with slip st to first tr: 24 tr and
6 ch-3 sps.

Rnd 3: Work Beginning Cluster, ch 2, (dc, ch 3,
dc) in next ch-3 sp, ch 2, ★ work Cluster, ch 2,
(dc, ch 3, dc) in next ch-3 sp, ch 2; repeat from ★
around; join with slip st to top of Beginning
Cluster, finish off: 18 sts and 18 sps.

HALF MOTIF (Make 16)
Ch 4; join with slip st to form a ring.

Row 1 (Right side)**:** Ch 5 **(counts as first dc plus
ch 2)**, dc in ring, (ch 2, dc in ring) twice; do **not**
join: 4 dc and 3 ch-2 sps.

Note: Mark Row 1 as **right** side.

Row 2: Ch 5 **(counts as first tr plus ch 1)**, turn;
4 tr in next ch-2 sp, (ch 3, 4 tr in next ch-2 sp)
twice, ch 1, tr in last dc: 14 tr and 4 sps.

Row 3: Ch 4 **(counts as first dc plus ch 1)**, turn;
dc in next ch-1 sp, ch 2, work Cluster, ch 2, ★ (dc,
ch 3, dc) in next ch-3 sp, ch 2, work Cluster, ch 2;
repeat from ★ once **more**, dc in next ch-1 sp,
ch 1, dc in last tr; finish off.

ASSEMBLY
Using Placement Diagram, page 137, as a guide
and working through **both** loops, whipstitch Motifs
and Half Motifs together forming 17 horizontal
strips **(Fig. 9a, page 144)**, beginning in center ch
of first ch-3 and ending in center ch of next ch-3;
then join strips together, beginning in first dc on
Half Motif and center ch of ch-3 on Motif and
ending in last dc on Half Motif and center ch of
next ch-3 on last Motif.

Continued on page 137.

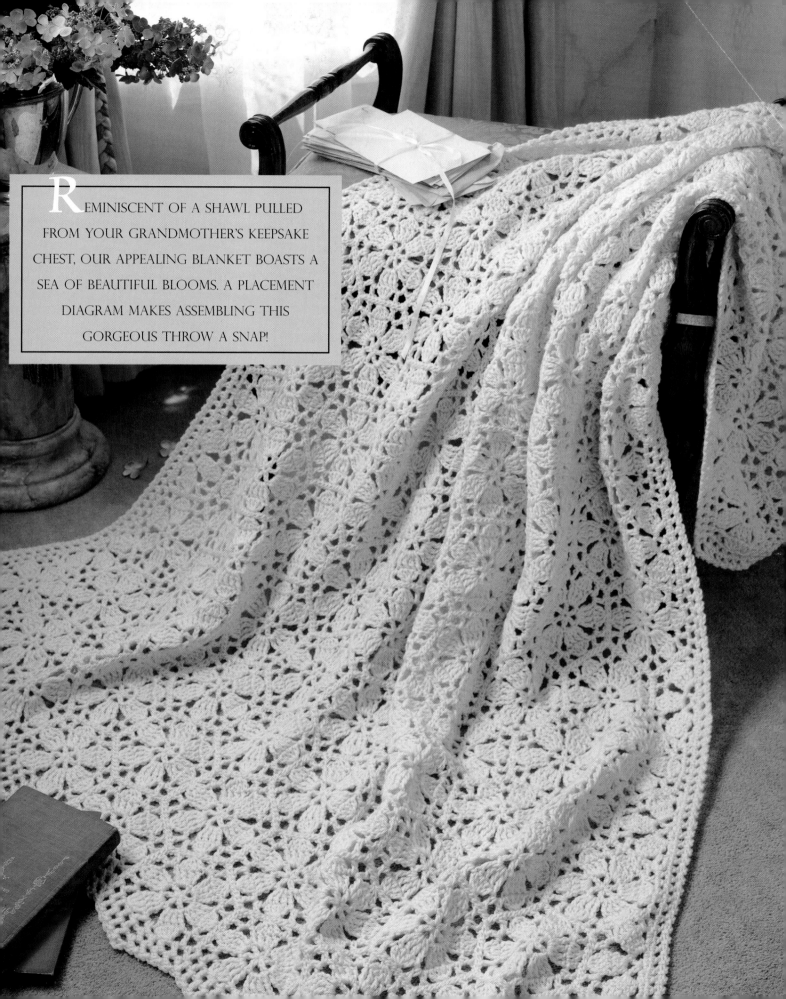

REMINISCENT OF A SHAWL PULLED
FROM YOUR GRANDMOTHER'S KEEPSAKE
CHEST, OUR APPEALING BLANKET BOASTS A
SEA OF BEAUTIFUL BLOOMS. A PLACEMENT
DIAGRAM MAKES ASSEMBLING THIS
GORGEOUS THROW A SNAP!

Gentle Moments

Finished Size: 52" x 70"

MATERIALS
Worsted Weight Yarn:
  38 ounces, (1,080 grams, 2,495 yards)
Crochet hook, size I (5.50 mm) **or** size needed
  for gauge
Yarn needle

GAUGE: Each Square = 6"

Gauge Swatch: 3" square
Work same as Square through Rnd 2.

STITCH GUIDE

TREBLE CROCHET *(abbreviated tr)*
YO twice, insert hook in st or sp indicated, YO and pull up a loop (4 loops on hook), (YO and draw through 2 loops on hook) 3 times.

DOUBLE TREBLE CROCHET
  (abbreviated dtr)
YO 3 times, insert hook in ch-5 sp indicated, YO and pull up a loop (5 loops on hook), (YO and draw through 2 loops on hook) 4 times.

BEGINNING CLUSTER (uses next 4 tr)
Ch 4, ★ YO twice, insert hook in **next** tr, YO and pull up a loop, (YO and draw through 2 loops on hook) twice; repeat from ★ 3 times **more**, YO and draw through all 5 loops on hook.

CLUSTER (uses next 5 tr)
★ YO twice, insert hook in **next** tr, YO and pull up a loop, (YO and draw through 2 loops on hook) twice; repeat from ★ 4 times **more**, YO and draw through all 6 loops on hook.

DECREASE
YO, insert hook in same ch as joining on **same** Square, YO and pull up a loop, YO and draw through 2 loops on hook, YO, insert hook in same ch as joining on **next** Square, YO and pull up a loop, YO and draw through 2 loops on hook, YO and draw through all 3 loops on hook **(counts as one dc)**.

SQUARE (Make 88)
Rnd 1 (Right side)**:** Ch 3, 11 hdc in third ch from hook; join with slip st to top of beginning ch-3: 12 sts.

Note: Loop a short piece of yarn around any stitch to mark Rnd 1 as **right** side.

Rnd 2: Ch 4 **(counts as first tr)**, tr in same st and in next hdc, 2 tr in next hdc, ch 5, ★ 2 tr in next hdc, tr in next hdc, 2 tr in next hdc, ch 5; repeat from ★ 2 times **more**; join with slip st to first tr: 20 tr and 4 ch-5 sps.

Rnd 3: Work Beginning Cluster, ch 3, (tr, ch 1, dtr, ch 3, dtr, ch 1, tr) in next ch-5 sp, ch 3, ★ work Cluster, ch 3, (tr, ch 1, dtr, ch 3, dtr, ch 1, tr) in next ch-5 sp, ch 3; repeat from ★ 2 times **more**; join with slip st to top of Beginning Cluster: 4 Clusters and 20 sps.

Rnd 4: Ch 3 **(counts as first dc, now and throughout)**, ★ † 3 dc in next ch-3 sp, dc in next tr, dc in next ch-1 sp and in next dtr, (2 dc, ch 3, 2 dc) in next ch-3 sp, dc in next dtr, dc in next ch-1 sp and in next tr, 3 dc in next ch-3 sp †, dc in next Cluster; repeat from ★ 2 times **more**, then repeat from † to † once; join with slip st to first dc, finish off: 68 dc and 4 ch-3 sps.

ASSEMBLY
Working through **inside** loops only, whipstitch Squares together forming 8 vertical strips of 11 Squares each *(Fig. 9b, page 144)*, beginning in center ch of first corner ch-3 and ending in center ch of next corner ch-3; then whipstitch strips together in same manner.

EDGING
Rnd 1: With **right** side facing, join yarn with slip st in any corner ch-3 sp; ch 3, (dc, ch 3, 2 dc) in same sp, ★ † dc in next 17 dc, (dc in next ch, decrease, dc in next ch and in next 17 dc) across to next corner ch-3 sp †, (2 dc, ch 3, 2 dc) in corner ch-3 sp; repeat from ★ 2 times **more**, then repeat from † to † once; join with slip st to first dc, do **not** finish off: 764 dc and 4 ch-3 sps.

Continued on page 137.

Captivating Cosmos

Finished Size: 53½" x 69½"

MATERIALS
Worsted Weight Yarn:
Black - 49 ounces, (1,390 grams, 2,770 yards)
Scraps - 20 ounces,
(570 grams, 1,130 yards) **total**
Note: We used 7 different colors.
Crochet hook, size H (5.00 mm) **or** size needed
for gauge

GAUGE: Each Motif = 5½"
(straight edge to straight edge)

Gauge Swatch: 2½" diameter
Work same as Motif through Rnd 2.

STITCH GUIDE

LONG SINGLE CROCHET (abbreviated LSC)
Insert hook in st indicated, YO and pull up a
loop even with loop on hook, YO and draw
through both loops on hook.

LONG DOUBLE CROCHET
(abbreviated LDC)
YO, insert hook in st or sp indicated, YO and
pull up a loop even with loop on hook, (YO
and draw through 2 loops on hook) twice.

PICOT
Ch 4, slip st in fourth ch from hook.

MOTIF (Make 111)
With color desired, ch 5; join with slip st to form a
ring.

Rnd 1 (Right side): Ch 1, 12 sc in ring; join with
slip st to first sc, finish off.

Note: Loop a short piece of yarn around any stitch
to mark Rnd 1 as **right** side.

Rnd 2: With **right** side facing, join color desired
with slip st in any sc; ch 3 **(counts as first dc, now
and throughout)**, 2 dc in same st, ch 1, skip next
sc, ★ 3 dc in next sc, ch 1, skip next sc; repeat
from ★ around; join with slip st to first dc,
finish off: 18 dc and 6 ch-1 sps.

Rnd 3: With **right** side facing, join color desired
with sc in first dc of any 3-dc group **(see Joining
With Sc, page 142)**; 2 sc in next dc, sc in next dc,
working **around** next ch-1 **(Fig. 6, page 143)**, work
LSC in skipped sc on Rnd 1, ★ sc in next dc, 2 sc
in next dc, sc in next dc, working **around** next
ch-1, work LSC in skipped sc on Rnd 1; repeat
from ★ around; join with slip st to first sc, do **not**
finish off: 30 sts.

Rnd 4: Working **around** sts on Rnd 3 and in dc
and ch-1 sps on Rnd 2, slip st in first dc, ch 3,
work 2 LDC in next dc, work LDC in next dc,
work LDC in next ch-1 sp **before** LSC and in same
sp **after** LSC, ★ work LDC in next dc, work 2 LDC
in next dc, work LDC in next dc, work LDC in
next ch-1 sp **before** LSC and in same sp **after** LSC;
repeat from ★ around; join with slip st to first dc,
finish off: 36 sts.

Rnd 5: With **right** side facing and working in Back
Loops Only of LDC **(Fig. 2, page 143)**, join Black
with sc in last LDC made; sc in next 2 sts, sc in sp
before next LDC **(Fig. 5, page 143)**, sc in next
3 LDC, working **around** Rnd 4, work LSC in **both**
loops of LSC on Rnd 3 **below**, ★ sc in next 3 LDC
on Rnd 4, sc in sp **before** next LDC, sc in next
3 LDC, working **around** Rnd 4, work LSC in **both**
loops of LSC on Rnd 3 **below**; repeat from ★
around; join with slip st to **both** x loops of first sc:
48 sts.

Rnd 6: Ch 3, working in both loops, dc in next
2 sc, (2 dc, ch 1, 2 dc) in next sc, ★ dc in next
7 sts, (2 dc, ch 1, 2 dc) in next sc; repeat from ★
around to last 4 sc, dc in last 4 sc; join with slip st
to first dc, finish off: 66 dc and 6 ch-1 sps.

HALF MOTIF (Make 12)
With Black, ch 13 **loosely**; place marker in third
ch from hook for st placement.

Row 1 (Right side): Dc in fourth ch from hook
(3 skipped chs count as first dc) and in each ch
across to last ch, 2 dc in last ch: 12 dc.

Note: Mark Row 1 as **right** side.

Rows 2-4: Ch 3, turn; dc in same st and in each
dc across to last dc, 2 dc in last dc; do **not**
finish off: 18 dc.

110

Continued on page 138.

Blooming Squares

Finished Size: 49" x 67"

MATERIALS
Worsted Weight Yarn:
Dk Green - 17½ ounces,
(500 grams, 990 yards)
Lt Rose - 14 ounces, (400 grams, 790 yards)
Lt Green - 10 ounces,
(280 grams, 565 yards)
Dk Rose - 9 ounces, (260 grams, 510 yards)
Crochet hook, size I (5.50 mm) **or** size needed
for gauge
Yarn needle

GAUGE: Each Square = 4½"

Gauge Swatch: 2½" diameter
Work same as Square through Rnd 2.

STITCH GUIDE

> **FRONT POST DOUBLE CROCHET**
> **(abbreviated FPdc)**
> YO, insert hook from **front** to **back** around
> post of st indicated **(Fig. 4, page 143)**, YO and
> pull up a loop (3 loops on hook), (YO and
> draw through 2 loops on hook) twice.

SQUARE (Make 140)
With Lt Rose, ch 5; join with slip st to form a ring.

Rnd 1 (Right side): Ch 3 **(counts as first dc)**, 15 dc
in ring; join with slip st to first dc: 16 dc.

Note: Loop a short piece of yarn around any stitch
to mark Rnd 1 as **right** side.

Rnd 2: Ch 1, sc in same st, work FPdc around next
dc, ch 1, ★ sc in next dc, work FPdc around next
dc, ch 1; repeat from ★ around; join with slip st to
first sc, finish off: 16 sts and 8 ch-1 sps.

Rnd 3: With **right** side facing, join Dk Rose with
slip st in any sc; ch 3, work FPdc around next
FPdc, ch 1, ★ hdc in next sc, ch 1, work FPdc
around next FPdc, ch 1; repeat from ★ around;
join with slip st to second ch of beginning ch-3,
finish off: 16 sts and 16 ch-1 sps.

Rnd 4: With **right** side facing, join Lt Green with
slip st in last ch-1 sp made; ch 6 **(counts as first
dc plus ch 3, now and throughout)**, dc in same
sp, ch 1, sc in next ch-1 sp, ch 1, slip st in next
ch-1 sp, ch 1, sc in next ch-1 sp, ch 1, ★ (dc,
ch 3, dc) in next ch-1 sp, ch 1, sc in next ch-1 sp,
ch 1, slip st in next ch-1 sp, ch 1, sc in next
ch-1 sp, ch 1; repeat from ★ 2 times **more**; join
with slip st to first dc, finish off: 20 sts and 20 sps.

Rnd 5: With **right** side facing, join Dk Green with
slip st in any corner ch-3 sp; ch 6, dc in same sp,
ch 1, dc in next dc, ch 1, (skip next ch, dc in next
st, ch 1) 4 times, ★ (dc, ch 3, dc) in next corner
ch-3 sp, ch 1, dc in next dc, ch 1, (skip next ch,
dc in next st, ch 1) 4 times; repeat from ★ 2 times
more; join with slip st to first dc, finish off: 28 dc
and 28 sps.

ASSEMBLY
With Dk Green, whipstitch Squares together
forming 10 vertical strips of 14 Squares each
(Fig. 9a, page 144), beginning in center ch of first
corner ch-3 and ending in center ch of next corner
ch-3; then whipstitch strips together in same
manner.

EDGING
Rnd 1: With **right** side facing, join Dk Green with
sc in any corner ch-3 sp **(see Joining With Sc,
page 142)**; ch 2, sc in same sp, ch 1, ★ (sc in next
sp, ch 1) across to next corner ch-3 sp, (sc, ch 2,
sc) in corner ch-3 sp, ch 1; repeat from ★ 2 times
more, (sc in next sp, ch 1) across; join with slip st
to first sc: 384 sps.

Rnd 2: Slip st in first corner ch-2 sp, ch 1, (sc,
ch 2, sc) in same sp, ch 1, ★ (sc in next ch-1 sp,
ch 1) across to next corner ch-2 sp, (sc, ch 2, sc)
in corner ch-2 sp, ch 1; repeat from ★ 2 times
more, (sc in next ch-1 sp, ch 1) across; join with
slip st to first sc, finish off.

Continued on page 139.

Spring Blossoms

Finished Size: 48" x 63"

MATERIALS
Worsted Weight Yarn:
39 ounces, (1,110 grams, 2,560 yards)
Crochet hook, size I (5.50 mm) **or** size needed
for gauge
Yarn needle

GAUGE: Each Square = 7¹/₂"

Gauge Swatch: 4" diameter
Work same as Square through Rnd 3.

STITCH GUIDE

TREBLE CROCHET (abbreviated tr)
YO twice, insert hook in ch-5 sp indicated, YO
and pull up a loop (4 loops on hook), (YO and
draw through 2 loops on hook) 3 times.

CLUSTER (uses next 6 dc)
★ YO, insert hook in **next** dc, YO and pull up
a loop, YO and draw through 2 loops on hook;
repeat from ★ 5 times **more**, YO and draw
through all 7 loops on hook. Push Cluster to
right side.

SQUARE (Make 48)
Ch 3; join with slip st to form a ring.

Rnd 1 (Right side)**:** Ch 3 **(counts as first dc, now
and throughout)**, 15 dc in ring; join with slip st to
first dc: 16 dc.

Note: Loop a short piece of yarn around any stitch
to mark Rnd 1 as **right** side.

Rnd 2: Working in Front Loops Only **(Fig. 2,
page 143)**, slip st in next dc, ch 3, 5 dc in same st,
★ ch 3, skip next dc, 6 dc in next dc; repeat from
★ around to last st, ch 1, skip last st, hdc in first dc
to form last ch-3 sp: 48 dc and 8 ch-3 sps.

Rnd 3: Sc in last ch-3 sp made, ch 3, working in
both loops, work Cluster, ★ ch 4, sc in next
ch-3 sp, ch 3, work Cluster; repeat from ★ around,
ch 1, dc in first sc to form last ch-4 sp: 8 Clusters
and 16 sps.

Rnd 4: Sc in last ch-4 sp made, (dc, ch 5, dc) in
next sc, sc in next ch-3 sp, ★ (ch 3, sc in next sp)
3 times, (dc, ch 5, dc) in next sc, sc in next
ch-3 sp; repeat from ★ 2 times **more**, (ch 3, sc in
next sp) twice, ch 1, hdc in first sc to form last
ch-3 sp.

Rnd 5: Ch 4 **(counts as first dc plus ch 1, now and
throughout)**, (3 tr, ch 3, 3 tr) in next ch-5 sp, ch 1,
dc in next ch-3 sp, ch 2, hdc in next ch-3 sp,
ch 2, ★ dc in next ch-3 sp, ch 1, (3 tr, ch 3, 3 tr)
in next ch-5 sp, ch 1, dc in next ch-3 sp, ch 2,
hdc in next ch-3 sp, ch 2; repeat from ★ 2 times
more; join with slip st to first dc: 36 sts and 20 sps.

Rnd 6: Ch 3, dc in next ch-1 sp and in next 3 tr,
(2 dc, ch 2, 2 dc) in next ch-3 sp, dc in next 3 tr
and in next ch-1 sp, (dc in next st, 2 dc in next
ch-2 sp) twice, ★ dc in next dc, dc in next ch-1 sp
and in next 3 tr, (2 dc, ch 2, 2 dc) in next ch-3 sp,
dc in next 3 tr and in next ch-1 sp, (dc in next st,
2 dc in next ch-2 sp) twice; repeat from ★ 2 times
more; join with slip st to first dc: 76 dc and
4 ch-2 sps.

Rnd 7: Ch 4, skip next dc, dc in next dc, ch 1,
skip next dc, dc in next 3 dc, (2 dc, ch 3, 2 dc) in
next ch-2 sp, dc in next 3 dc, ch 1, skip next dc,
★ (dc in next dc, ch 1, skip next dc) 6 times, dc in
next 3 dc, (2 dc, ch 3, 2 dc) in next ch-2 sp, dc in
next 3 dc, ch 1, skip next dc; repeat from ★
2 times **more**, (dc in next dc, ch 1, skip next dc) 4
times; join with slip st to first dc, finish off: 64 dc
and 32 sps.

ASSEMBLY
Working through **both** loops, whipstitch Squares
together forming 6 vertical strips of 8 Squares each
(Fig. 9a, page 144), beginning in center ch of first
corner ch-3 and ending in center ch of next corner
ch-3; then whipstitch strips together in same
manner.

EDGING
Rnd 1: With **right** side facing, join yarn with slip st
in any corner ch-3 sp; ch 3, (dc, ch 3, 2 dc) in

Continued on page 139.

Afternoon Tea

Finished Size: 51" x 65"

MATERIALS
Worsted Weight Yarn:
43 ounces, (1,220 grams, 2,680 yards)
Crochet hook, size I (5.50 mm) **or** size needed
for gauge
Yarn needle

GAUGE: Each Square = 7"

Gauge Swatch: 4" square
Work same as Square through Rnd 2.

STITCH GUIDE

TREBLE CROCHET *(abbreviated tr)*
YO twice, insert hook in st indicated, YO and
pull up a loop (4 loops on hook), (YO and
draw through 2 loops on hook) 3 times.

2-TR CLUSTER (uses one st)
★ YO twice, insert hook in st indicated, YO
and pull up a loop, (YO and draw through
2 loops on hook) twice; repeat from ★ once
more, YO and draw through all 3 loops on
hook.

3-TR CLUSTER (uses one st)
★ YO twice, insert hook in st indicated, YO
and pull up a loop, (YO and draw through
2 loops on hook) twice; repeat from ★ 2 times
more, YO and draw through all 4 loops on
hook.

SQUARE (Make 63)
Rnd 1 (Right side)**:** Ch 2, 8 sc in second ch from
hook; join with slip st to first sc.

Note: Loop a short piece of yarn around any stitch
to mark Rnd 1 as **right** side.

Rnd 2: Ch 3, work 2-tr Cluster in same st, ch 4,
work 2-tr Cluster in fourth ch from hook, ch 5,
work 2-tr Cluster in fourth ch from hook, work
3-tr Cluster in next sc, ★ ch 5, work 3-tr Cluster in

next sc, ch 4, work 2-tr Cluster in fourth ch from
hook, ch 5, work 2-tr Cluster in fourth ch from
hook, work 3-tr Cluster in next sc; repeat from ★
2 times **more**, ch 2, dc in top of first 2-tr Cluster to
form last ch-5 sp: 16 Clusters and 4 ch-5 sps.

Rnd 3: Ch 7, tr in top of joining dc, ch 2, skip next
2 Clusters, work (3-tr Cluster, ch 7, 3-tr Cluster) in
next ch, ch 2, skip next 2 Clusters, ★ (tr, ch 3, tr)
in center ch of next ch-5, ch 2, skip next
2 Clusters, work (3-tr Cluster, ch 7, 3-tr Cluster) in
next ch, ch 2, skip next 2 Clusters; repeat from ★
2 times **more**; join with slip st to fourth ch of
beginning ch-7: 16 sts and 16 sps.

Rnd 4: Ch 3 **(counts as first dc, now and
throughout)**, 3 dc in next ch-3 sp, dc in next tr,
2 dc in next ch-2 sp, dc in next Cluster, (4 dc,
ch 3, 4 dc) in next ch-7 sp, dc in next Cluster,
2 dc in next ch-2 sp, ★ dc in next tr, 3 dc in next
ch-3 sp, dc in next tr, 2 dc in next ch-2 sp, dc in
next Cluster, (4 dc, ch 3, 4 dc) in next ch-7 sp, dc
in next Cluster, 2 dc in next ch-2 sp; repeat from
★ 2 times **more**; join with slip st to first dc,
finish off: 76 dc and 4 ch-3 sps.

ASSEMBLY
Working through **both** loops, whipstitch Squares
together forming 7 vertical strips of 9 Squares each
(Fig. 9a, page 144), beginning in center ch of first
corner ch-3 and ending in center ch of next corner
ch-3; then whipstitch strips together in same
manner.

EDGING
Rnd 1: With **right** side facing, join yarn with slip st
in any corner ch-3 sp; ch 3, (dc, ch 3, 2 dc) in
same sp, ★ † dc in next 19 dc, (dc in next sp and
in same ch as joining on same Square, dc in same
ch as joining on next Square and in next sp, dc in
next 19 dc) across to next corner ch-3 sp †, (2 dc,
ch 3, 2 dc) in corner ch-3 sp; repeat from ★
2 times **more**, then repeat from † to † once; join
with slip st to first dc, do **not** finish off: 736 dc and
4 ch-3 sps.

Continued on page 139.

Finished Size: 48$\frac{1}{2}$" x 65"

MATERIALS

Worsted Weight Yarn:
Yellow - 24 ounces, (680 grams, 1,355 yards)
Blue - 15 ounces, (430 grams, 850 yards)
Dk Blue - 11 ounces, (310 grams, 620 yards)
Ecru - 8 ounces, (230 grams, 450 yards)
Crochet hook, size I (5.50 mm) **or** size needed for gauge
Yarn needle

GAUGE: Each Square = 5$\frac{1}{2}$"

Gauge Swatch: 2$\frac{3}{4}$" diameter
Work same as Square through Rnd 2.

STITCH GUIDE

TREBLE CROCHET (abbreviated tr)
YO twice, insert hook in st indicated, YO and pull up a loop (4 loops on hook), (YO and draw through 2 loops on hook) 3 times.

BEGINNING CLUSTER (uses one sc)
Ch 2, ★ YO, insert hook in **same** st, YO and pull up a loop, YO and draw through 2 loops on hook; repeat from ★ once **more**, YO and draw through all 3 loops on hook.

CLUSTER (uses one sc)
★ YO, insert hook in sc indicated, YO and pull up a loop, YO and draw through 2 loops on hook; repeat from ★ 2 times **more**, YO and draw through all 4 loops on hook.

DECREASE
Pull up a loop in next 2 sc, YO and draw through all 3 loops on hook.

SQUARE (Make 88)

Rnd 1 (Right side)**:** With Yellow, ch 2, 8 sc in second ch from hook; join with slip st to first sc.

Note: Loop a short piece of yarn around any stitch to mark Rnd 1 as **right** side.

Rnd 2: Work Beginning Cluster, ch 3, (work Cluster in next sc, ch 3) around; join with slip st to top of Beginning Cluster, finish off: 8 Clusters and 8 ch-3 sps.

Rnd 3: With **right** side facing, join Ecru with sc in any ch-3 sp *(see Joining With Sc, page 142)*; 4 sc in same sp, 5 sc in next ch-3 sp and in each ch-3 sp around; join with slip st to first sc, finish off: 40 sc.

Rnd 4: With **right** side facing, join Blue with sc in center sc of any 5-sc group; sc in same st and in next sc, decrease, sc in next sc, ★ 2 sc in next sc, sc in next sc, decrease, sc in next sc; repeat from ★ around; join with slip st to first sc, finish off.

Rnd 5: With **right** side facing, join Dk Blue with sc in any decrease; sc in next 2 sc, hdc in next sc, dc in next sc, (tr, ch 3, tr) in next decrease, dc in next sc, hdc in next sc, ★ sc in next 5 sts, hdc in next sc, dc in next sc, (tr, ch 3, tr) in next decrease, dc in next sc, hdc in next sc; repeat from ★ 2 times **more**, sc in last 2 sc; join with slip st to first sc, finish off: 44 sts and 4 ch-3 sps.

Rnd 6: With **wrong** side facing, join Blue with sc in any corner ch-3 sp; ch 3, sc in same sp, ch 1, skip next tr, (sc in next st, ch 1, skip next st) 5 times, ★ (sc, ch 3, sc) in next corner ch-3 sp, ch 1, skip next tr, (sc in next st, ch 1, skip next st) 5 times; repeat from ★ 2 times **more**; join with slip st to first sc, finish off: 28 sc and 28 sps.

Rnd 7: With **right** side facing, join Yellow with sc in any corner ch-3 sp; ch 3, sc in same sp and in next sc, [working **behind** next ch-1 *(Fig. 6, page 143)*, dc in skipped st one rnd **below**, sc in next sc] 6 times, ★ (sc, ch 3, sc) in next corner ch-3 sp, sc in next sc, (working **behind** next ch-1, dc in skipped st one rnd **below**, sc in next sc) 6 times; repeat from ★ 2 times **more**; join with slip st to first sc, finish off: 60 sts and 4 ch-3 sps.

Continued on page 140.

Finished Size: 50" x 68"

MATERIALS
Worsted Weight Brushed Acrylic Yarn:
Blue - 39 ounces, (1,110 grams, 1,755 yards)
Cream - 37 ounces, (1,050 grams, 1,665 yards)
Crochet hook, size H (5.00 mm) **or** size needed
for gauge

GAUGE SWATCH: 6" square
Work same as Square.

STITCH GUIDE

FRONT POST DOUBLE CROCHET
   (abbreviated FPdc)
YO, insert hook from **front** to **back** around
post of st indicated *(Fig. 4, page 143)*, YO and
pull up a loop (3 loops on hook), (YO and
draw through 2 loops on hook) twice. Skip st
behind FPdc.

FRONT POST TREBLE CROCHET
   (abbreviated FPtr)
YO twice, insert hook from **front** to **back**
around post of dc indicated *(Fig. 4, page 143)*,
YO and pull up a loop (4 loops on hook), (YO
and draw through 2 loops on hook) 3 times.
Skip st behind FPtr.

SQUARE (Make 88)
Rnd 1 (Right side): With Cream, ch 4, 11 dc in
fourth ch from hook; join with slip st to top of
beginning ch: 12 sts.

Note: Loop a short piece of yarn around any stitch
to mark Rnd 1 as **right** side.

Rnd 2: Ch 1, sc in same st, ch 5, skip next 2 dc,
(sc in next dc, ch 5, skip next 2 dc) around; join
with slip st to first sc: 4 ch-5 sps.

Rnd 3: Slip st in first ch-5 sp, ch 3 **(counts as first
dc, now and throughout)**, 5 dc in same sp, ch 1,
(6 dc in next ch-5 sp, ch 1) around; join with
slip st to first dc, finish off: 24 dc.

Rnd 4: With **right** side facing, join Blue with sc in
any ch-1 sp *(see Joining With Sc, page 142)*; ch 6,
skip next 3 dc, sc in sp **before** next dc *(Fig. 5,
page 143)*, ch 6, ★ sc in next ch-1 sp, ch 6, skip
next 3 dc, sc in sp **before** next dc, ch 6; repeat
from ★ around; join with slip st to first sc:
8 ch-6 sps.

Rnd 5: Slip st in first ch-6 sp, ch 3, (3 dc, ch 2,
4 dc) in same sp, dc in next ch-6 sp, work FPtr
around second dc to **right** of next ch-1 sp on
Rnd 3, dc in same ch-6 sp as last dc made,
★ (4 dc, ch 2, 4 dc) in next ch-6 sp, dc in next
ch-6 sp, work FPtr around second dc to **right** of
next ch-1 sp on Rnd 3, dc in same ch-6 sp as last
dc made; repeat from ★ around; join with slip st
to first dc, finish off: 40 dc.

Rnd 6: With **right** side facing, join Cream with
slip st in any corner ch-2 sp; ch 3, 4 dc in same
sp, dc in next 5 dc, work FPdc around next FPtr,
dc in next 5 dc, ★ 5 dc in next ch-2 sp, dc in next
5 dc, work FPdc around next FPtr, dc in next
5 dc; repeat from ★ around; join with slip st to first dc,
finish off: 60 dc.

Rnd 7: With **right** side facing, join Blue with slip st
in center dc of any corner 5-dc group; ch 3, (2 dc,
ch 2, 3 dc) in same st, dc in Back Loop Only of
next 7 dc *(Fig. 2, page 143)*, work FPdc around
next FPdc, dc in Back Loop Only of next 7 dc,
★ (3 dc, ch 2, 3 dc) in **both** loops of next dc, dc in
Back Loop Only of next 7 dc, work FPdc around
next FPdc, dc in Back Loop Only of next 7 dc;
repeat from ★ around; join with slip st to first dc,
finish off: 80 dc.

ASSEMBLY
Join Squares together forming 8 vertical strips of
11 Squares each as follows:

Holding two Squares with **wrong** sides together
and working through **inside** loops of **both** pieces,
join Cream with sc in second ch of first corner
ch-2; sc in each st across to first ch of next corner
ch-2, sc in first ch; finish off.

Join strips in same manner.

Continued on page 140.

RESEMBLING DOZENS OF PRETTY LITTLE
PACKAGES, THE SQUARE MOTIFS ON THIS SNUG
AFGHAN ARE HIGHLIGHTED BY THREE-DIMENSIONAL
FLOWERS. OUR JOINING TECHNIQUE FRAMES
EACH BLOCK, AND THE WRAP IS FINISHED
WITH SIMPLE EDGING.

Poppies

Finished Size: 55" x 69"

MATERIALS

Worsted Weight Yarn:
Green - 17 ounces, (480 grams, 1,120 yards)
Ecru - 16 ounces, (450 grams, 1,055 yards)
Rose - 12 ounces, (340 grams, 790 yards)
Dk Rose - 11 ounces, (310 grams, 725 yards)
Grey - 1 ounce, (30 grams, 65 yards)
Crochet hook, size I (5.50 mm) **or** size needed
for gauge
Yarn needle

GAUGE SWATCH: 7" square
Work same as Square.

STITCH GUIDE

TREBLE CROCHET (abbreviated tr)
YO twice, insert hook in sp indicated, YO and
pull up a loop (4 loops on hook), (YO and
draw through 2 loops on hook) 3 times.

DECREASE (uses 2 dc)
Insert hook in skipped dc **below** next ch-3, YO
and pull up a loop, skip **next** 2 ch-3 sps, insert
hook in skipped dc **below** next ch-3, YO and
pull up a loop, YO and draw through all
3 loops on hook **(counts as one sc)**.

SQUARE (Make 63)

Rnd 1 (Right side)**:** With Dk Rose, ch 2, sc in
second ch from hook, ch 5, (sc in same st, ch 5) 5
times; join with slip st to first sc: 6 ch-5 sps.

Note: Loop a short piece of yarn around any stitch
to mark Rnd 1 as **right** side.

Rnd 2: Slip st in first ch-5 sp, ch 1, (sc, ch 1, 7 dc,
ch 1, sc) in same sp **(Petal made)** and in each
ch-5 sp around; join with slip st to first sc:
6 Petals.

Rnd 3: Ch 3, skip next ch-1 sp, slip st in next dc,
ch 3, (skip next dc, slip st in next dc, ch 3) 3

times, skip next ch-1 sp and next sc, ★ slip st in
next sc, ch 3, skip next ch-1 sp, slip st in next dc,
ch 3, (skip next dc, slip st in next dc, ch 3) 3
times, skip next ch-1 sp and next sc; repeat from ★
around; join with slip st to base of beginning ch-3,
finish off: 30 ch-3 sps.

Rnd 4: With **right** side facing, working **behind**
ch-3 **(Fig. 6, page 143)** and in skipped dc on
Rnd 2, join Green with sc in dc **below** ch-3 at
center top of any Petal **(see Joining With Sc,
page 142)**; ch 2, decrease, ch 2, ★ sc in dc **below**
next ch-3, ch 2, decrease, ch 2; repeat from ★
around; join with slip st to first sc: 12 ch-2 sps.

Rnd 5: Ch 2, 2 hdc in same st, ch 1, dc in next sc,
(2 tr, ch 3, 2 tr) in next ch-2 sp, dc in next sc,
ch 1, ★ 3 hdc in next sc, ch 1, dc in next sc, (2 tr,
ch 3, 2 tr) in next ch-2 sp, dc in next sc, ch 1;
repeat from ★ around; join with slip st to top of
beginning ch-2: 12 sps.

Rnd 6: Slip st in next 2 hdc and in next ch-1 sp,
ch 3 **(counts as first dc, now and throughout)**,
2 dc in same sp, ch 1, (3 dc, ch 3, 3 dc) in next
ch-3 sp, ch 1, ★ (3 dc in next ch-1 sp, ch 1) twice,
(3 dc, ch 3, 3 dc) in next ch-3 sp, ch 1; repeat
from ★ 2 times **more**, 3 dc in last ch-1 sp, ch 1;
join with slip st to first dc, finish off: 16 sps.

Rnd 7: With **right** side facing, join Rose with
slip st in any ch-3 sp; ch 3, (2 dc, ch 3, 3 dc) in
same sp, ch 1, (3 dc in next ch-1 sp, ch 1) across
to next ch-3 sp, ★ (3 dc, ch 3, 3 dc) in ch-3 sp,
ch 1, (3 dc in next ch-1 sp, ch 1) across to next
ch-3 sp; repeat from ★ around; join with slip st to
first dc, finish off: 20 sps.

Rnd 8: With Ecru, repeat Rnd 7: 24 sps.

CENTER

With 2 fingers held together side by side, wind
Grey **loosely** and **evenly** around fingers 5 times.
Carefully slip the yarn off fingers and firmly tie a
10" length of yarn around middle. Leave yarn ends
long enough to attach the Center. Clip the loops
on both ends and trim as desired. Attach Center to
Flower and secure ends.

Continued on page 141.

Dotted With Flowers

Finished Size: 48" x 70"

MATERIALS
Worsted Weight Yarn:
57 ounces, (1,620 grams, 3,585 yards)
Crochet hooks, sizes H (5.00 mm) **and** I
(5.50 mm) **or** sizes needed for gauge
Yarn needle

GAUGE: With larger size hook,
16 dc = 5" and 7 rows = 4"

Gauge Swatch: 5"w x 4"h
With larger size hook, ch 18 **loosely**.
Row 1: Dc in fourth ch from hook **(3 skipped chs count as first dc)** and in each ch across: 16 dc.
Rows 2-7: Ch 3 **(counts as first dc)**, turn; dc in next dc and in each dc across.
Finish off.

STITCH GUIDE

CLUSTER
★ YO, insert hook in sc indicated, YO and pull up a loop, YO and draw through 2 loops on hook; repeat from ★ 3 times **more**, YO and draw through all 5 loops on hook. Push Cluster to **right** side.

AFGHAN

With larger size hook, ch 148 **loosely**.

Row 1 (Right side)**:** Sc in second ch from hook and in each ch across: 147 sc.

Note: Loop a short piece of yarn around any stitch to mark Row 1 as **right** side.

Row 2: Ch 1, turn; sc in first 2 sc, work Cluster in next sc, (sc in next 2 sc, work Cluster in next sc) across to last 3 sc, sc in last 3 sc: 48 Clusters.

Row 3: Ch 1, turn; sc in each st across: 147 sc.

Row 4: Ch 1, turn; sc in first 3 sc, (work Cluster in next sc, sc in next 2 sc) across: 48 Clusters.

Row 5: Ch 1, turn; sc in each st across: 147 sc.

Rows 6 and 7: Repeat Rows 2 and 3.

Rows 8 and 9: Ch 3 **(counts as first dc, now and throughout)**, turn; dc in next st and in each st across.

Row 10: Ch 3, turn; dc in next 16 sts, ch 1, ★ skip next dc, dc in next 15 sts, ch 1; repeat from ★ 6 times **more**, skip next dc, dc in last 17 sts: 139 dc and 8 ch-1 sps.

Row 11: Ch 3, turn; dc in next 14 sts, ch 1, skip next dc, dc in next 3 sts, ch 1, ★ skip next dc, dc in next 11 sts, ch 1, skip next dc, dc in next 3 sts, ch 1; repeat from ★ 6 times **more**, skip next dc, dc in last 15 sts: 131 dc and 16 ch-1 sps.

Row 12: Ch 3, turn; dc in next 12 sts, ch 1, ★ skip next dc, dc in next 7 sts, ch 1; repeat from ★ 14 times **more**, skip next dc, dc in last 13 sts.

Row 13: Ch 3, turn; dc in next 10 sts, ch 1, skip next dc, dc in next 11 sts, ch 1, ★ skip next dc, dc in next 3 sts, ch 1, skip next dc, dc in next 11 sts, ch 1; repeat from ★ 6 times **more**, skip next dc, dc in last 11 sts.

Row 14: Ch 3, turn; dc in next 8 dc, ch 1, ★ skip next dc, dc in next 15 sts, ch 1; repeat from ★ 7 times **more**, skip next dc, dc in last 9 dc: 138 dc and 9 ch-1 sps.

Row 15: Repeat Row 13.

Row 16: Repeat Row 12.

Row 17: Repeat Row 11.

Row 18: Repeat Row 10.

Rows 19 and 20: Ch 3, turn; dc in next dc and in each st across: 147 dc.

Row 21: Ch 1, turn; sc in each dc across.

Rows 22-147: Repeat Rows 2-21, 6 times; then repeat Rows 2-7 once **more**.

Do **not** finish off.

Continued on page 141.

Finished Size: 45¹/₂" x 63"

MATERIALS

Worsted Weight Yarn:
   35 ounces, (990 grams, 2,296 yards)
Crochet hook, size I (5.50 mm) **or** size needed
   for gauge

GAUGE: In pattern, one repeat
            and 11 rows = 6"

Gauge Swatch: 11¹/₂"w x 6"h
Ch 48.
Work same as Afghan Body for 11 rows.
Finish off.

STITCH GUIDE

PUFF STITCH (abbreviated Puff St)
★ YO, insert hook in ch-1 sp indicated, YO
and pull up a loop even with loop on hook;
repeat from ★ 2 times **more** (7 loops on hook),
YO and draw through 6 loops on hook, YO
and draw through remaining 2 loops on hook.

SHELL
(2 Dc, ch 2, 2 dc) in sp indicated.

AFGHAN BODY

Ch 120.

Row 1: Sc in second ch from hook, ch 3, skip next
3 chs, sc in next 2 chs, ch 2, skip next 2 chs, sc in
next ch, ch 1, skip next 2 chs, (dc, ch 1) 3 times in
next ch, skip next 2 chs, sc in next ch, ch 2, skip
next 2 chs, sc in next 2 chs, ★ ch 5, skip next
4 chs, sc in next ch, ch 5, skip next 4 chs, sc in
next 2 chs, ch 2, skip next 2 chs, sc in next ch,
ch 1, skip next 2 chs, (dc, ch 1) 3 times in next ch,
skip next 2 chs, sc in next ch, ch 2, skip next
2 chs, sc in next 2 chs; repeat from ★ across to
last 4 chs, ch 3, skip next 3 chs, sc in last ch:
51 sts and 40 sps.

Row 2 (Right side)**:** Ch 5 **(counts as first dc plus
ch 2, now and throughout)**, turn; 2 dc in next sc,
ch 2, 2 dc in next sc, skip next ch-2 sp, work
Puff St in next ch-1 sp, (ch 3, work Puff St in next
ch-1 sp) 3 times, skip next ch-2 sp, 2 dc in next

sc, ch 2, 2 dc in next sc, ★ ch 3, (sc in next
ch-5 sp, ch 3) twice, 2 dc in next sc, ch 2, 2 dc in
next sc, skip next ch-2 sp, work Puff St in next
ch-1 sp, (ch 3, work Puff St in next ch-1 sp) 3
times, skip next ch-2 sp, 2 dc in next sc, ch 2,
2 dc in next sc; repeat from ★ across to last
ch-3 sp, ch 2, skip last ch-3 sp, dc in last sc:
39 sps.

Row 3: Ch 5, turn; skip first ch-2 sp, work Shell in
next ch-2 sp, ch 2, sc in next ch-3 sp, (ch 3, sc in
next ch-3 sp) twice, ch 2, work Shell in next
ch-2 sp, ★ ch 5, skip next ch-3 sp, sc in next
ch-3 sp, ch 5, skip next ch-3 sp, work Shell in
next ch-2 sp, ch 2, sc in next ch-3 sp, (ch 3, sc in
next ch-3 sp) twice, ch 2, work Shell in next
ch-2 sp; repeat from ★ across to last ch-2 sp, ch 2,
skip last ch-2 sp, dc in last dc: 40 sps.

Row 4: Ch 5, turn; work Shell in next Shell
(ch-2 sp), ch 5, skip next ch-2 sp, sc in next
ch-3 sp, ch 3, sc in next ch-3 sp, ch 5, work Shell
in next Shell, ★ ch 3, (sc in next ch-5 sp, ch 3)
twice, work Shell in next Shell, ch 5, skip next
ch-2 sp, sc in next ch-3 sp, ch 3, sc in next
ch-3 sp, ch 5, work Shell in next Shell; repeat
from ★ across to last ch-2 sp, ch 2, skip last
ch-2 sp, dc in last dc: 39 sps.

Row 5: Ch 5, turn; work Shell in next Shell, ch 2,
sc in next ch-5 sp, ch 1, (dc, ch 1) 3 times in next
ch-3 sp, sc in next ch-5 sp, ch 2, work Shell in
next Shell, ★ ch 5, skip next ch-3 sp, sc in next
ch-3 sp, ch 5, work Shell in next Shell, ch 2, sc in
next ch-5 sp, ch 1, (dc, ch 1) 3 times in next
ch-3 sp, sc in next ch-5 sp, ch 2, work Shell in
next Shell; repeat from ★ across to last ch-2 sp,
ch 2, skip last ch-2 sp, dc in last dc: 50 sps.

Row 6: Ch 5, turn; work Shell in next Shell, skip
next ch-2 sp, work Puff St in next ch-1 sp, (ch 3,
work Puff St in next ch-1 sp) 3 times, work Shell in
next Shell, ★ ch 3, (sc in next ch-5 sp, ch 3) twice,
work Shell in next Shell, skip next ch-2 sp, work
Puff St in next ch-1 sp, (ch 3, work Puff St in next
ch-1 sp) 3 times, work Shell in next Shell; repeat
from ★ across to last ch-2 sp, ch 2, skip last
ch-2 sp, dc in last dc; do **not** finish off: 39 sps.

Continued on page 128.

DELICATE AND AIRY, THIS SOFT
GREEN WRAP IS A GORGEOUS WAY TO GET
COZY ON A COOL EVENING. PUFF STITCHES
AND SHELLS CREATE THE ILLUSION OF
BUDDING LEAVES AND PETALS.

Row 7: Ch 5, turn; work Shell in next Shell, ch 2, sc in next ch-3 sp, (ch 3, sc in next ch-3 sp) twice, ch 2, work Shell in next Shell, ★ ch 5, skip next ch-3 sp, sc in next ch-3 sp, ch 5, work Shell in next Shell, ch 2, sc in next ch-3 sp, (ch 3, sc in next ch-3 sp) twice, ch 2, work Shell in next Shell; repeat from ★ across to last ch-2 sp, ch 2, skip last ch-2 sp, dc in last dc: 40 sps.

Repeat Rows 4-7 until Afghan Body measures approximately 47" from beginning ch, ending by working Row 6.

Last Row: Ch 1, turn; sc in first dc, ch 3, 2 sc in next Shell, ch 2, sc in next ch-3 sp, (ch 3, sc in next ch-3 sp) twice, ch 2, 2 sc in next Shell, ★ ch 4, skip next ch-3 sp, dc in next ch-3 sp, ch 4, 2 sc in next Shell, ch 2, sc in next ch-3 sp, (ch 3, sc in next ch-3 sp) twice, ch 2, 2 sc in next Shell; repeat from ★ across to last ch-2 sp, ch 3, skip last ch-2 sp, sc in last dc; do **not** finish off: 30 sps.

EDGING

Rnd 1: Ch 1, turn; 2 sc in first sc, † 3 sc in next sp, sc in next 2 sts, 2 sc in next sp, (sc in next st, 2 sc in next sp) 3 times, sc in next 2 sts, ★ 4 sc in next sp, 2 sc in next st, 4 sc in next sp, sc in next 2 sts, 2 sc in next sp, (sc in next st, 2 sc in next sp) 3 times, sc in next 2 sts; repeat from ★ across to last sp, 3 sc in last sp and in last st; work 201 sc evenly spaced across end of rows †; working in free loops *(Fig. 3b, page 143)* and in sps across beginning ch, 3 sc in ch at base of first sc, repeat from † to † once, sc in same st as first sc; join with slip st to first sc: 656 sc.

Rnd 2: Ch 1, do **not** turn; sc in same st, ch 5, skip next 3 sc, (sc in next sc, ch 5, skip next 3 sc) across to center sc of next corner 3-sc group, ★ (sc, ch 5) twice in center sc, skip next 3 sc, (sc in next sc, ch 5, skip next 3 sc) across to center sc of next corner 3-sc group; repeat from ★ 2 times **more**, sc in same st as first sc, ch 5; join with slip st to first sc: 168 ch-5 sps.

Rnd 3: Slip st in next 2 chs, ch 1, sc in same sp, ★ (ch 5, sc in next ch-5 sp) across to next corner ch-5 sp, (ch 5, sc) twice in corner ch-5 sp; repeat from ★ around, ch 2, dc in first sc to form last ch-5 sp: 172 ch-5 sps.

Rnds 4 and 5: Ch 1, sc in last ch-5 sp made, ★ (ch 5, sc in next ch-5 sp) across to next corner ch-5 sp, (ch 5, sc) twice in corner ch-5 sp; repeat from ★ around, ch 2, dc in first sc to form last ch-5 sp: 180 ch-5 sps.

Rnd 6: Ch 1, sc in last ch-5 sp made, ch 5, ★ (sc in next ch-5 sp, ch 5) across to next corner ch-5 sp, (sc, ch 5) twice in corner ch-5 sp; repeat from ★ around; join with slip st to first sc: 184 ch-5 sps.

Rnd 7: Slip st in first ch-5 sp, ch 3, (dc, ch 2, 2 dc) in same sp, ch 2, sc in next ch-5 sp, ch 1, † (dc, ch 1) 3 times in next ch-5 sp, sc in next ch-5 sp, ch 2, work Shell in next ch-5 sp, ch 2, sc in next ch-5 sp, ch 1 †; repeat from † to † across to next corner ch-5 sp, (dc, ch 1) 7 times in corner ch-5 sp, sc in next ch-5 sp, ch 2, ★ work Shell in next ch-5 sp, ch 2, sc in next ch-5 sp, ch 1, repeat from † to † across to next corner ch-5 sp, (dc, ch 1) 7 times in corner ch-5 sp, sc in next ch-5 sp, ch 2; repeat from ★ 2 times **more**; join with slip st to top of beginning ch-3: 338 sps.

Rnd 8: Slip st in next dc, slip st in next ch and in same ch-2 sp, ch 5, 2 dc in same sp, † skip next ch-2 sp, work Puff St in next ch-1 sp, (ch 3, work Puff St in next ch-1 sp) 3 times, skip next ch-2 sp, work Shell in next Shell †; repeat from † to † across to within one ch-2 sp of next corner 7-dc group, skip next ch-2 sp, work Puff St in next ch-1 sp, (ch 3, work Puff St in next ch-1 sp) 7 times, skip next ch-2 sp, ★ work Shell in next Shell, repeat from † to † across to within one ch-2 sp of next corner 7-dc group, skip next ch-2 sp, work Puff St in next ch-1 sp, (ch 3, work Puff St in next ch-1 sp) 7 times, skip next ch-2 sp; repeat from ★ 2 times **more**, dc in same sp as first dc; join with slip st to first dc: 200 sps.

Rnd 9: Slip st in next ch and in same ch-2 sp, ch 5, 2 dc in same sp, ch 2, † sc in next ch-3 sp, (ch 3, sc in next ch-3 sp) twice, ch 2, work Shell in next Shell, ch 2 †; repeat from † to † across to next corner Puff St group, sc in next ch-3 sp, (ch 3, sc in next ch-3 sp) 6 times, ch 2, ★ work Shell in next Shell, ch 2, repeat from † to † across to next corner Puff St group, sc in next ch-3 sp, (ch 3, sc in next ch-3 sp) 6 times, ch 2; repeat from ★ 2 times **more**, dc in same sp as first dc; join with slip st to first dc: 246 sps.

Rnd 10: Slip st in next ch and in same ch-2 sp, ch 5, 2 dc in same sp, ch 5, skip next ch-2 sp, sc in next ch-3 sp, ch 3, sc in next ch-3 sp, ch 5, ★ † skip next ch-2 sp, work Shell in next Shell, ch 5, skip next ch-2 sp, sc in next ch-3 sp, ch 3, sc in next ch-3 sp, ch 5 †; repeat from † to † across to within one ch-3 sp of next corner sc, work Shell in next 2 ch-3 sps, ch 5, sc in next ch-3 sp, ch 3, sc in next ch-3 sp, ch 5; repeat from ★ around to last ch-2 sp, skip last ch-2 sp, dc in same sp as first dc; join with slip st to first dc: 204 sps.

Rnd 11: Slip st in next ch and in same ch-2 sp, ch 5, 2 dc in same sp, ★ † ch 2, sc in next ch-5 sp, ch 1, (dc, ch 1) 3 times in next ch-3 sp, sc in next ch-5 sp, ch 2, work Shell in next Shell †; repeat from † to † across to second Shell of next corner 2-Shell group, ch 3, work Shell in next Shell; repeat from ★ around to last 3 sps, ch 2, sc in next ch-5 sp, ch 1, (dc, ch 1) 3 times in next ch-3 sp, sc in last ch-5 sp, ch 2, dc in same sp as first dc; join with slip st to first dc: 358 sps.

Rnd 12: Slip st in next ch and in same ch-2 sp, ch 5, 2 dc in same sp, ★ † skip next ch-2 sp, work Puff St in next ch-1 sp, (ch 3, work Puff St in next ch-1 sp) 3 times, skip next ch-2 sp, work Shell in next Shell †; repeat from † to † across to next corner ch-3 sp, ch 3, (sc, ch 3) twice in corner ch-3 sp, work Shell in next Shell; repeat from ★ 3 times **more**, skip next ch-2 sp, work Puff St in next ch-1 sp, (ch 3, work Puff St in next ch-1 sp) 3 times, skip last ch-2 sp, dc in same sp as first dc; join with slip st to first dc: 216 sps.

Rnd 13: Slip st in next ch and in same ch-2 sp, ch 5, 2 dc in same sp, ch 2, sc in next ch-3 sp, (ch 3, sc in next ch-3 sp) twice, ch 2, ★ work Shell in next Shell, ch 2, sc in next ch-3 sp, (ch 3, sc in next ch-3 sp) twice, ch 2; repeat from ★ around, dc in same sp as first dc; join with slip st to first dc: 270 sps.

Rnd 14: Slip st in next ch and in same ch-2 sp, ch 5, 2 dc in same sp, ch 5, skip next ch-2 sp, sc in next ch-3 sp, ch 3, sc in next ch-3 sp, ch 5, skip next ch-2 sp, ★ work Shell in next Shell, ch 5, skip next ch-2 sp, sc in next ch-3 sp, ch 3, sc in next ch-3 sp, ch 5, skip next ch-2 sp; repeat from ★ around, dc in same sp as first dc; join with slip st to first dc: 216 sps.

Rnd 15: Slip st in next ch and in same ch-2 sp, ch 5, 2 dc in same sp, ch 2, sc in next ch-5 sp, ch 1, ★ † (dc, ch 1) 3 times in next ch-3 sp, sc in next ch-5 sp, ch 2, work Shell in next Shell, ch 2, sc in next ch-5 sp, ch 1 †; repeat from † to † across to next corner ch-3 sp, (dc, ch 1) 7 times in corner ch-3 sp, sc in next ch-5 sp, ch 2, work Shell in next Shell, ch 2, sc in next ch-5 sp, ch 1; repeat from ★ 3 times **more**, (dc, ch 1) 3 times in next ch-3 sp, sc in last ch-5 sp, ch 2, dc in same sp as first dc; join with slip st to first dc: 394 sps.

Rnd 16: Slip st in next ch and in same ch-2 sp, ch 5, 2 dc in same sp, ★ † skip next ch-2 sp, work Puff St in next ch-1 sp, (ch 3, work Puff St in next ch-1 sp) 3 times, skip next ch-2 sp, work Shell in next Shell †; repeat from † to † across to within one ch-2 sp of next corner 7-dc group, skip next ch-2 sp, work Puff St in next ch-1 sp, (ch 3, work Puff St in next ch-1 sp) 7 times, skip next ch-2 sp, work Shell in next Shell; repeat from ★ 3 times **more**, skip next ch-2 sp, work Puff St in next ch-1 sp, (ch 3, work Puff St in next ch-1 sp) 3 times, skip next ch-2 sp, dc in same sp as first dc; join with slip st to first dc: 232 sps.

Rnd 17: Slip st in first ch-2 sp, ch 1, sc in same sp, (ch 5, sc in next sp) around, ch 2, dc in first sc to form last ch-5 sp.

Rnd 18: Ch 1, sc in last ch-5 sp made, ch 5, sc in third ch from hook, ch 2, ★ sc in next ch-5 sp, ch 5, sc in third ch from hook, ch 2; repeat from ★ around; join with slip st to first sc, finish off.

Design by Terry Kimbrough.

ROYAL ROSES
Continued from page 88.

Rnd 3: (Slip st, ch 2, slip st) in first corner ch-3 sp, ★ † ch 1, (slip st in next ch-1 sp, ch 1) across to next corner ch-3 sp †, (slip st, ch 2, slip st) in corner ch-3 sp; repeat from ★ 2 times **more**, then repeat from † to † once; join with slip st to first slip st, finish off.

Design by Anne Halliday.

SWEET VIOLETS

Continued from page 90.

Row 1: Ch 4 **(counts as first dc plus ch 1, now and throughout)**, skip first Cluster, work (Puff St, ch 3, Puff St) in top of next Cluster **(4-Petal group complete)**, ch 1, ★ skip next ch-1 sp and next Cluster, work (Puff St, ch 3, Puff St) in top of next Cluster **(4-Petal group complete)**, ch 1; repeat from ★ across to last ch, dc in last ch; finish off: 77 sps.

Row 2: With **right** side facing, join Green with slip st in first dc; ch 2 **(counts as first hdc, now and throughout)**, hdc in next ch-1 sp, 3 hdc in next ch-3 sp, ★ hdc in next Puff St, hdc in next ch-1 sp and in next Puff St, 3 hdc in next ch-3 sp; repeat from ★ across to last Puff St, skip last Puff St, hdc in next ch-1 sp and in last dc; finish off: 229 hdc.

Row 3: With **right** side facing, join Purple with slip st in first hdc; ch 3 **(counts as first dc, now and throughout)**, skip next hdc, work Beginning 2-Petal group, (ch 4, work 4-Petal group) across to last 4 hdc, work 2-Petal group, skip next hdc, dc in last hdc; do **not** finish off: 37 4-Petal groups and 2 2-Petal groups.

Row 4: Ch 4, turn; work Puff St in center of next 2-Petal group, ch 1, ★ work (Puff St, ch 3, Puff St) in center of next 4-Petal group, ch 1; repeat from ★ across to last 2-Petal group, work Puff St in center of last 2-Petal group, ch 1, dc in last dc; finish off: 77 sps.

Row 5: With **right** side facing, join Green with slip st in first dc; ch 2, (hdc in next ch-1 sp and in next Puff St) twice, ★ 3 hdc in next ch-3 sp, hdc in next Puff St, hdc in next ch-1 sp and in next Puff St; repeat from ★ across to last ch-1 sp, hdc in last ch-1 sp and in last dc; finish off: 229 hdc.

Row 6: With **right** side facing, join Lt Purple with slip st in first hdc; ch 7, place marker in fifth ch from hook for st placement, work Beginning 4-Petal group, (ch 4, work 4-Petal group) across to last hdc, ch 1, dc in last hdc; do **not** finish off: 38 4-Petal groups.

Row 7: Ch 4, turn; skip next ch-1 sp, ★ work (Puff St, ch 3, Puff St) in center of next 4-Petal group, ch 1, skip next ch-1 sp; repeat from ★ across to marked ch, dc in marked ch; finish off: 77 sps.

Row 8: With **right** side facing, join Ecru with slip st in first dc; ch 2, hdc in next ch-1 sp, 3 hdc in next ch-3 sp, ★ hdc in next Puff St, hdc in next ch-1 sp and in next Puff St, 3 hdc in next ch-3 sp; repeat from ★ across to last Puff St, skip last Puff St, hdc in next ch-1 sp and in last dc; do **not** finish off: 229 hdc.

Row 9: Ch 2, turn; hdc in Front Loop Only of next hdc and each hdc across **(Fig. 2, page 143)**.

Row 10: Ch 2, turn; hdc in Back Loop Only of next hdc and each hdc across.

Rows 11-14: Repeat Rows 9 and 10 twice.

Finish off.

Row 15: With **right** side facing and working in both loops, join Lt Purple with slip st in first hdc; ch 7, place marker in fifth ch from hook for st placement, work Beginning 4-Petal group, (ch 4, work 4-Petal group) across to last hdc, ch 1, dc in last hdc; do **not** finish off: 38 4-Petal groups.

Row 16: Ch 4, turn; skip next ch-1 sp, ★ work (Puff St, ch 3, Puff St) in center of next 4-Petal group, ch 1, skip next ch-1 sp; repeat from ★ across to marked ch, dc in marked ch; finish off: 77 sps.

Row 17: With **right** side facing, join Green with slip st in first dc; ch 2, hdc in next ch-1 sp, 3 hdc in next ch-3 sp, ★ hdc in next Puff St, hdc in next ch-1 sp and in next Puff St, 3 hdc in next ch-3 sp; repeat from ★ across to last Puff St, skip last Puff St, hdc in next ch-1 sp and in last dc; finish off: 229 hdc.

Rows 18-66: Repeat Rows 3-17, 3 times; then repeat Rows 3-6 once **more**.

Row 67: Ch 4, turn; ★ work (Puff St, ch 3, slip st, ch 3, Puff St) in center of next 4-Petal group, ch 1; repeat from ★ across to marked ch, dc in marked ch; finish off.

Trim: With **right** side facing and working in sts across Foundation Row, join Lt Purple with slip st in ch at base of first dc; ch 4, ★ work (Puff St, ch 3, slip st, ch 3, Puff St) in center of next 4-Petal group, ch 1, skip next ch-1 sp; repeat from ★ across to last ch, dc in last ch; finish off.

Holding 8 strands of Ecru yarn together, each 15" long, add fringe evenly across short edges of Afghan **(Figs. 11c & d, page 144)**.

Design by Rena Stevens.

PRETTY POSIES

Continued from page 92.

Rnd 2: With **right** side facing, join Lt Rose with dc in fourth ch-1 sp **after** joining; dc in same sp, † ch 1, skip next 2 dc, dc in next dc, ch 1, (2 dc, ch 1) twice in next ch-1 sp, skip next dc, dc in next dc, ch 1, dc in next ch-1 sp, ch 1, skip next 2 dc, dc in next dc, ch 1, (2 dc, ch 1) twice in next ch-1 sp, skip next dc, dc in next dc, ch 1, skip next 2 dc, ★ dc in sp **before** next joining, ch 1, skip next slip st and next 2 sc, working **around** next sc **(Fig. 6, page 143)**, work LSC in same ch as sc (between legs), ch 1, skip next 2 sc and next slip st, dc in sp **before** next dc on next Motif, ch 1, skip next 2 dc, dc in next dc, ch 1, (2 dc, ch 1) twice in next ch-1 sp, skip next dc, dc in next dc, ch 1, dc in next ch-1 sp, ch 1, skip next 2 dc, dc in next dc, ch 1, (2 dc, ch 1) twice in next ch-1 sp, skip next dc, dc in next dc, ch 1, skip next 2 dc; repeat from ★ 11 times **more** †, 2 dc in next ch-1 sp, repeat from † to † once; join with slip st to first dc, finish off.

Rnd 3 (Joining rnd): With **right** side facing, join Green with dc in second ch-1 sp **before** joining; † (ch 1, dc in next ch-1 sp) 3 times, dc in next 2 dc, (dc, tr, ch 1, tr, dc) in next ch-1 sp, dc in next 2 dc and in next ch-1 sp, (ch 1, dc in next ch-1 sp) 3 times, dc in next 2 dc, (dc, tr, ch 1, tr, dc) in next ch-1 sp, dc in next 2 dc, ★ hdc in next ch-1 sp, ch 1, hdc in next ch-1 sp, skip next dc and next ch-1 sp, working **around** next LSC, work LSC in same ch as LSC (between legs), skip next ch-1 sp and next dc, hdc in next ch-1 sp, working in corresponding sts on **previous Motif**, work Joining in last hdc made, ch 1, hdc in next ch-1 sp on **new Motif**, work Joining in next hdc on **previous Motif**, (dc in next dc on **new Motif**, work Joining in next dc on **previous Motif**) twice, dc in next ch-1 sp on **new Motif**, work Joining in next dc on **previous Motif**, tr in same sp on **new Motif**, work Joining in next tr on **previous Motif**, ch 1, (tr, dc) in same sp on **new Motif**, dc in next 2 dc and in next ch-1 sp, (ch 1, dc in next ch-1 sp) 3 times, dc in next 2 dc, (dc, tr, ch 1, tr, dc) in next ch-1 sp, dc in next 2 dc; repeat from ★ 11 times **more** †, dc in next ch-1 sp, repeat from † to † once; join with slip st to first dc, finish off.

Rnd 4: With **right** side facing and working across short edge of Strip, join White with sc in first corner ch-1 sp **(see Joining With Sc, page 142)**; † sc in next tr and in each st and each ch-1 sp across to next corner ch-1 sp, (sc, ch 2, sc) in corner ch-1 sp, ★ sc in next tr and in each st and each ch-1 sp across to next joining, decrease, sc in same sp as second leg of decrease just made; repeat from ★ 11 times **more**, sc in next tr and in each st and each ch-1 sp across to next corner ch-1 sp †, (sc, ch 2, sc) in corner ch-1 sp, repeat from † to † once, sc in same sp as first sc, hdc in first sc to form last ch-2 sp; do **not** finish off: 500 sc and 4 ch-2 sps.

Rnd 5: Ch 3, [(dc, ch 1) 3 times, 2 dc] in last ch-2 sp made, skip next 2 sc, sc in next sc, skip next 2 sc, ★ [(2 dc, ch 1, 2 dc) in next sc, skip next 2 sc, sc in next sc, skip next 2 sc] across to next corner ch-2 sp, [2 dc, ch 1, (dc, ch 1) twice, 2 dc] in corner ch-2 sp, skip next 2 sc, sc in next sc, skip next 2 sc; repeat from ★ 2 times **more**, [(2 dc, ch 1, 2 dc) in next sc, skip next 2 sc, sc in next sc, skip next 2 sc] across; join with slip st to first dc, finish off.

REMAINING 6 STRIPS

The method used to connect the Strips is a no-sew joining also known as "join-as-you-go". After the First Strip is made, each remaining Strip is worked through Rnd 4, then crocheted together as Rnd 5 is worked **(Fig. 10, page 144)**.

Work same as First Strip through Rnd 4: 500 sc and 4 ch-2 sps.

Rnd 5 (Joining rnd): Ch 4, 2 dc in last ch-2 sp made, skip next 2 sc, sc in next sc, skip next 2 sc, [(2 dc, ch 1, 2 dc) in next sc, skip next 2 sc, sc in next sc, skip next 2 sc] across to next corner ch-2 sp, ★ [2 dc, ch 1, (dc, ch 1) twice, 2 dc] in corner ch-2 sp, skip next 2 sc, sc in next sc, skip next 2 sc, [(2 dc, ch 1, 2 dc) in next sc, skip next 2 sc, sc in next sc, skip next 2 sc] across to next corner ch-2 sp; repeat from ★ once **more**, (2 dc, ch 1, dc) in corner ch-2 sp, holding Strips with **wrong** sides together, slip st in corresponding corner ch-1 sp on **previous Strip**, (dc, ch 1, 2 dc) in same sp on **new Strip**, skip next 2 sc, sc in next sc, skip next 2 sc, † 2 dc in next sc, slip st in corresponding ch-1 sp on **previous Strip**, 2 dc in same st on **new Strip**, skip next 2 sc, sc in next sc, skip next 2 sc †; repeat from † to † across, (2 dc, ch 1, dc) in same corner ch-2 sp as beginning ch-4, skip next ch-1 sp on **previous Strip**, slip st in next ch-1 sp; join with slip st to third ch of beginning ch-4 on **new Strip**, finish off.

Design by Lesli Phillips.